Hear Us NOW!

*How to Ask Questions and
Connect with Children
So They Feel Heard*

Carmen Kotto M.Ed.

To contact the author,
Email: hearusnow2020@gmail.com

ISBN # 978-1-7369916-0-2 (Paperback)

Edited by Lisa Carnicum and Patricia Pedroza

Book design by Deborah Perdue, Illumination Graphics

DEDICATION

This book is dedicated to George Floyd, whom I have never met but have seen many times in my dreams.

He no longer has a voice, but WE do!

Special thanks to:

Mr. and Mrs. Zimmerman, who have supported me for years even though we have never met. With their support and encouragement, my students have had all of the necessary items needed for success in school.

I would also like to thank the O & O Academy faculty for their wisdom, knowledge, and meditations. I have learned so much and have been able to share it with my students. This book is possible only because of them.

I am so grateful to my former student Cesar Anaya who is on a journey to make the world a better place and to Sal Khan for creating Khan Academy.

I am also very thankful to my school and administration for allowing me to be me.

SPECIAL NOTE:

This book is easily digestible as a life-nutritional supplement in a busy person's schedule. You can read it as a meal or as a series of snacks. It repeats key themes and words throughout. The purpose is to rewire your neural synapses via the "magic" of repetition in a way that an ordinary, more succinct book would not. The words and concepts will easily become a part of your thought processes, serving you as reminders. All human brains – not only busy ones – benefit from this method.

Disclaimer:

Some names and identifying details have been changed to protect the privacy of individuals. Some genders of the students and identifying details have been changed to protect the privacy of individuals.

This book is designed to provide information and motivation to our readers. It is sold with the understanding that the publisher is not engaged to render any type of psychological, legal, or any other kind of professional advice. The content of each section is the sole expression and opinion of its author, and not necessarily that of the publisher. No warranties or guarantees are expressed or implied by the publisher's choice to include any of the content in this volume. Neither the publisher nor the individual author(s) shall be liable for any physical, psychological, emotional, financial, or commercial damages, including, but not limited to, special, incidental, consequential, or other damages. Our views and rights are the same: You are responsible for your own choices, actions, and results.

CONTENTS

*"I wanted to talk about it. Damn it. I wanted to scream. I wanted to yell. I wanted to shout about it. But all I could do was whisper,'
'I'm fine.'"*
– Unknown

Although the author of this quote is unknown, many of our current students feel that exact sentiment.

INTRODUCTION

Hi everyone. I am a math teacher. You might be wondering . . . .

Why is a math teacher writing a book about students and their feelings? I am sharing these insights and reflections so that other teachers and parents can further understand what is going on inside the hearts and minds of our students! The hope is that you will learn how to connect with your students at a deeper, more profound level and help prevent students from coming out of this pandemic, social distancing, and distance learning ordeal in a state of depression, disconnection, and / or hopelessness. We have to be proactive and help our students now!

Depression is a feeling of loneliness and disconnection from the world around us. Many students are feeling these emotions, and it is exasperated by distance learning and everything else that they are experiencing right now. If we do not help them now, we will have an epidemic of depression among our youth later. Now is the time to be present for them. To fix the problem before it happens. NOW.

"300 million people today are globally recognized as suffering from depression.
By 2030, depression will be the biggest epidemic the world has ever known."
– World Health Organization

I have seen so many teachers burn out and stop caring. I am here to remind us that we have to care about the students we are entrusted to teach! I understand the burnout, but we need to find ways to keep falling in love with teaching. I still love teaching! I feel that this year is even more special with distance learning.

I have realized that part of my excitement comes from the deep connections that I have made with all of my students. Connections that, even now, help them to be successful during these difficult times. I do want to note that I am neither a psychologist nor a therapist. I have been teaching for over 30 years, and one of my areas of expertise is understanding how to connect with students.

I will share my insights and thoughts with you from a place of compassion. I want to encourage you to pause, wonder, and notice what your students are really feeling and saying. It will be very beneficial to you and your students to pay close attention.

I will share my findings on what students really need now and how you, as their teacher or parent, can provide that. For example, students need to feel like they are not alone, that they are empowered and entitled to their feelings, and that they are being heard. Building connections is the key, and I want to show teachers how to do just that. Many teachers struggle to build connections either because they do not know how to connect, or because they believe it is not necessary. I am here to claim that it is, in fact, desperately needed.

Have you ever spent a whole semester still trying to learn the names of your students? I am not proud to admit it, but that was me a few years ago. I did not realize how disconnected I was from the students. It took someone pointing it out for me to finally notice. At that major turning point, I had already been teaching for 26 years! This book is to help you become more aware, a wake-up call so you can, in turn, positively affect and change the lives of all of your students (and non-students) that you come into contact with.

A few questions you might want to ask yourself: Do you want to make a difference in a child's life? Do you want students to come back years later to visit and tell you the impact that you made in their lives? Do you want to hear them say, "You helped me more than you know!" Or perhaps, "You were the only teacher who made me feel seen, heard, and worthy!"

Connecting with students goes way beyond curriculum. Curriculum is important, but that should come after you establish a deep, heartfelt connection with your students. I am going to guide you through the process of how to connect. It may be strange or uncomfortable at first but, in time, it will become more natural for you and for your students.

The main goals for this book are for students to feel connected, and to have compassion for themselves as well as others. The words that I am writing are coming from my heart. The topics, questions, and responses flow naturally while talking with my students. Nothing is contrived. I simply ask a question and they share their feelings and thoughts while I listen attentively. At times, I feel the need to share back by offering some advice. Usually, I just let them know that they are not alone. A simple act that is incredibly important. Even the students who do not share, benefit from this. Students can see that others are feeling the same way, and thus beginning to heal their hearts. They will feel connected and heard.

Many people, including adults, appear happy on the outside. On the inside, an entirely different picture might be painted; they might even be screaming on the inside. I will share a little about one of my students from the beginning of this school year. She is eleven years old and is trying her best to do all of her work. Keep in mind that this is during a pandemic, doing distance learning, having record heat waves, and being surrounded by ash in the air from multiple fires. In online class (on Zoom), she appears to be so happy. I never thought anything was wrong. Then her mom emailed to say that she had always been an "A" student in the past. However, lately she has not been doing her work, and she has been acting very rebellious.

I followed up with a Zoom call with my student. She told me that she only pretends to be happy so her friends will think she is fine. She covers up the fact that she is stressed and does not know how to cope. We cried together. I talked her through it and will continue to keep an eye on her. These heartfelt conversations have turned her around, and she is now excelling again.

Teachers need to know that we are much more than adults delivering information to adolescents. For some students, we are the closest thing they have to a parent. Building connections with students is the most important action we can do to help them during this pandemic and throughout their lives. We do not know what is going on with students until they open up and tell us. In turn, they will not tell us unless they have a connection with us.

CONNECTING THROUGH MEDITATION

One strategy for building deeper connections with students is the art of meditation. I am very fortunate to work at a school where meditating with my students is encouraged. We spend three minutes a day deep-breathing and noticing our emotions. Implementing this was a very slow process. I needed the students to trust me in order for them to close their eyes and meditate. For two whole weeks, we only shut our eyes and focused on our breathing for a minute at a time. Then, the next couple of weeks we progressed to two minutes. Once I noticed that the students were able to keep their eyes closed, stay still, and do the deep-breathing exercises, I taught them how to do a meditation called "Serene Mind" by Preetha Ji, Co-founder of O & O Academy.

There are also several resources and guided meditations for students on Khan Academy and YouTube. I alternate between "Serene Mind" and a listening meditation. Listening meditations are when students are asked to close their eyes, sit very still, and just listen. Similar to when first implementing this practice, we started with just one minute and slowly increased the time to up to three minutes. After we finish, I ask them to share what they heard. It is interesting to see the progression of their responses with more practice.

CONNECTING
WITH THE AUTHOR

In order to understand my thoughts and gain your trust, I will share my background and experiences. I was born in Bolivia, just like Jaime Escalante, and raised in Alaska. I have a Bachelor of Arts in Elementary Education and Spanish. I have a Master of Arts in Secondary Education. I am currently working on my Doctorate equivalent, from India, in Human Development and Philosophy. It is a learning journey that will never end.

I started teaching Spanish at the high school and college levels in South Carolina. Then I moved to California, where I taught bilingual first grade. Later, I moved to teaching middle school. Middle school is the locus of that dreaded group of children, seen as half-developed humans or puberty-infested adolescents, that I absolutely adore! I also taught at a pre-school. In sum, I have taught from pre-school to college, and mentored teachers for a year. Mentoring teachers almost made me leave the teaching profession altogether, giving me yet another reason to write this book.

During my thirty-year career, I have always worked at schools that are predominantly socioeconomically disadvantaged. Schools where there are high percentages of second-language learners and special education students. Schools where the majority of students are one to two years below grade-level standards. Schools where I feel I am needed the most.

I currently teach seventh-grade math at a sixth- through twelfth-grade charter school where 84% qualify for free or reduced lunch, 97.7% are Latinx, and many are the first generation in their family to go to college. Many of the students have not yet learned to be self-motivated, adding another reason why building connections with them is incredibly powerful.

Teaching is not only my profession and career; it is my passion. Along my path, I have won several awards. Although listing them like a resume makes me a bit uncomfortable, as it can be perceived as bragging, it provides context and helps establish trust. In 1991, I was nominated for Teacher of the Year. In 2007, I was Teacher of the Year.

I have been featured in the newspaper twice for my unique teaching style. The first time was in 2006, in an article named "Atypical Tools." The second time was in 2007, in an article named "Dancing + Singing + Games = Unconventional Learning."

In 2015, I was the Comcast All-Star Teacher of the Year for California, where my school received a $20,000 grant. I had the honor of being on live TV to receive my award and hang out at the A's baseball field. I had the opportunity to meet and hug Madison Bumgarner (MVP 2014) and feel like a rock star!

In 2017, my class was featured on the Khan Academy website to promote Learn Storm. I was privileged to meet the founder of Khan Academy, Mr. Sal Khan. Furthermore, I won the Excellence in Teaching at Ceiba College Prep for the 2017-2018 year after being nominated by one of my students. In 2019, I was nominated by a fellow colleague for the Sanford Teacher Award.

Far superior to any award, the largest reward comes from students who find me, connect with me, and tell me that I was the reason they graduated years later. Former students who express to me that I was the only one who listened to them. Students who simply want to thank me.

For example, "D", a former student, found me and said, "You were the only teacher I actually remember. You listened. You were there for me. I appreciate that." Another student shared with me that he felt like he could do anything.

Along with my student's feelings of success and empowerment, they have consistently scored very high on the California State Testing compared with students from similar demographics in the district and state. Last year, my seventh-graders scored almost 20% higher than the state average and 36% higher than the district average. I attribute a huge part of their incredible scores to my connections with them. I was able to teach them effectively, and the students were able to learn efficiently. Proving that being one to two years below grade level, being socioeconomically disadvantaged, and the first generation to go to college are not obstacles for success. My students were able to score higher than the State of California averages. These huge successes would be impossible to achieve without building the connections that are indispensable to effective learning.

Deep, heartfelt connections not only allow teaching to run more smoothly, but also make classroom management much easier. Teachers can notice right away who is struggling, have more time to spare, gain more confidence, finish more curriculum, and have more energy at the end of each day. Students listen more, behave better in class, are less defiant, are more creative and engaged, and have higher test scores. Classes are more calm and productive. You fall in love with teaching (even distance learning). Everyone becomes all-around happier human beings.

Even though this book is about connecting with your students, I have included a section on my discipline procedures because building connections is interconnected with every part of being a teacher, even discipline. If the students feel like you hear and respect them, then they will work for you.

I, like many teachers, struggled with classroom management when I first started. I aspired to be better. The life-learner in me knew how to accomplish that. I took several classroom management seminars and read many books, including Fred Jones' *Tools for Teaching*, Dr. Harry Wong's *The First Days of School*, Jay Mathews' *Escalante: The Best Teacher in America*, Dr. Anita Archer's seminars, and other seminars on assertive-discipline and cooperative learning.

Jaime Escalante (the math teacher on whom the 1988 movie "Stand and Deliver" was based) was my hero. My teaching style is similar to his. All of my strategies and techniques are only further enhanced by connecting with my students. Throughout my career, I have varied my motivation methods, from handing out stickers and candy to putting marbles in a jar and rewarding them with pizza, but none of them long-term. It was way too much work for too little reward. Asking questions and actively listening to them, on the other hand, is very little work with huge rewards!

Teachers have asked me so many times, "Why aren't the students learning? Why aren't the students listening to me?" The truth is that lack of connection makes many students unmotivated to listen when we are teaching. Every teacher, regardless of the number of years you have been teaching, can start asking the right type of questions to enhance what you are already doing. Modifying your questions to give you opportunities to listen to your students works well for all subgroups of students, including English-language learners, students with learning disabilities, high-achieving students, low-achieving students, and middle-of-the-road students.

STARTING CONNECTIONS

You might be asking yourself "How can I start to connect with my students?" The first step is to acknowledge that you are not connected to your students, or not as connected as you would like to be. Be aware without judgement. We need to start connecting by listening to the children. This means taking the time to ask students deep, open-ended questions and giving them an opportunity to share their true feelings. Do this daily **without a script,** so that it can be genuine.

These questions are suggestions for you, but are not intended to be a script or a forced curriculum. Make the questions as natural as you can, and flow organically. It is all about creating a true connection so that the child feels safe, confident, and accepted. They need to both understand and feel that we care about them.

Regardless of how many years you have been teaching, asking kids questions and listening to them will make a world of difference to them. It really matters that they feel they matter.

Lastly, it is important to understand a little bit of adolescent psychology. You will notice how building connections develops self-esteem, sense of belonging, confidence, ease of learning, desire to learn, enjoyment of math (or any subject area), and wanting to attend class.

You will notice the students becoming more self-motivated, responsible, willing to cooperate, comfortable with making mistakes, and willing to ask for help. Feeling connected also makes the students experience many sensations that they might not be able to put into words themselves, such as pride, connection, accomplishment, equality, and inclusion.

REFERENCES

Preethaji (2018). Serene Mind. Retrieved from https://www.youtube.com/watch?v=OXg8xcWBMuo.

Gratitude **Meditation:** https://www.breathingroom.com/videos/feel-gratitude [I modify it for children and I guide it.]

QUARTER ONE

September 1, 2020 (Week 5 of School – Distance Learning)

A month has passed and I have been struggling to have my students do their work and to pay attention in class. It hit me like a ton of bricks that my students are stressed and cannot focus. They think that no one understands what they are going through. Pandemic, record heat, smoky air, distance learning, not being able to socialize, and so much more that I do not even know is a difficult equation that adds up to their inability to focus. I have several students who are dealing with deaths in their family and one child that had a seizure, fell, and sustained a concussion.

I wanted the students to know that they are not alone. That is why I started heartfelt conversations with them. My first question was, "How do you feel?" The answers I got were, "good, fine, bad, tired." So I asked them the next day, "How do you really feel?" They gave me the same answers because they did not know how they really felt. The following is how the heartfelt conversations began.

QUESTION
What can you do to raise your grade?
Actual student responses (without any corrections)
– *Try to participate more in class.*
– *Turn in the assignments on time.*
– *I could pay more attention.*
– *I can start doing all my missing assignments and asking for help.*

QUESTION
What are you struggling with in school?
Actual student responses (without any corrections)
– *Focusing.*
– *I'm struggling with doing my work.*
– *I am struggling with doing all the work from classes and working from home.*
– *I'm struggling to keep up with my work.*

QUESTION
Why do you think you are struggling?
Actual student responses (without any corrections)
– *Sometimes I get distracted and stressed.*
– *I think I struggle because most of the time I am not confident and I think that I don't know how to do the work.*
– *I think I am struggling because I procrastinate.*
– *I'm struggling because I can't focus.*
– *Well mine is still no excuse but the past two weeks my great grandma has been on hospice or however you spell it and I've been over there almost every day.*

MY INSIGHTS
I read many of their written responses out loud, without their names. I made general comments such as, "I am so sorry that you are going

through this," and "I wish you did not have to experience this." I could tell that it made them feel more comfortable with sharing and then they were willing to share more. While many students opened up, I noticed some were still cautious about sharing. I thanked every one of them for being so open, brave, and willing to share. At this point, I am only trying to get them to be comfortable and open up, at their own pace.

When I felt that they were ready to hear some advice, I said to them, "Stop being so hard on yourself. I know that you are doing the best you can in a very difficult situation." Sometimes it is not about helping them with strategies but, rather, it is about the students feeling heard. They will start to realize that what they are feeling is just like everyone else, making them feel more connected to the teacher, and even to their own feelings. They will know that they are okay and that they are not the only one going through these experiences.

HOMEWORK
Look into someone's eyes when you are talking. Notice how it feels.
This homework was not graded, and was only a suggestion.
Most did it.

September 8, 2020 (Week 6 of School – Distance Learning)
One of my main struggles during distance learning was that the students were not looking at me when I was teaching. If they are not looking at me, they are distracted and not learning. So, I gave my students a homework assignment yesterday on being in the present moment and making eye contact.

QUESTION
Did you look into someone's eyes when you are talking?
How did it feel?
Actual student responses (without any corrections)
– *Yes and it was really awkward.*

15

– When I was talking to my mom I looked into her eyes,It felt weird.
– Yes, I notice things about them that I never noticed before and it made it interesting
– I looked at my mom in the eyes and I felt more connected and this time I felt more comfortable.
– I did it and it was really awkward and uncomfortable.

MY INSIGHTS

I am trying to have my students be more in the present moment. Let's face it, many students are worried about what could happen in the future or they are preoccupied with what happened in the past. If we can teach them and if they can learn to be in the present moment, they would not be so afraid, worried, or stressed.

It is important to have students begin to notice their feelings. Once they start to notice them, then they can start to talk about them. There they can start to realize that others feel the same way, building their confidence because they know that their feelings are valid. Students feel more connected, confident, and comfortable. This is a great way for students to free themselves from feeling lonely and depressed when the pandemic is over. Slowly dissolving their discomfort and insecurities helps them to be in the moment.

HOMEWORK

Notice if someone is looking at you in your eyes when you are talking or when they are talking. How does it feel?

September 8, 2020 (Week 6 of School – Distance Learning)

QUESTION

Homework from the previous day: Did you notice when someone was looking in your eyes when you were talking? How did it feel? Actual student responses (without any corrections)

– Yes, it felt like if I was understanding the conversation more than before.

– I did notice and it made me feel validated and noticed.

– Yes when my mom looked at me in the eyes and I did to I felt like if i was getting more attention

– i did it made my mind go like you can see me and made me feel important

– It felt good because I felt like they were actually listening to me.

– I did notice someone look into my eyes when I was talking and it felt like they cared.

MY INSIGHTS

I wanted the students to realize that looking into someone's eyes means that they are in the present moment and that they really matter. Some students may not feel like they do matter to anyone perhaps because they have never noticed or felt it before. Eye contact can be meaningful and help them feel like they belong and are connected.

After the students began noticing how they felt when someone was looking at them, I asked them, "How do you think teachers feel when you don't look at them?" You should have seen their faces! They said, "They don't feel important, they think that we don't care, and we are not listening." I told them that teachers have the same feelings as any other human beings. Your parents also have the same feelings as you do, so just stop to notice. This discussion is not about making the students feel bad. It is about having them become aware of their actions, emotions, and feelings.

Again, these conversations are about helping students notice their feelings and helping them understand that these feelings are normal. If they begin to comprehend that they have similar feelings as everyone else, then they can begin to truly understand that there is more that unites us. It is another step towards combating students feeling lonely and depressed when the pandemic is over.

QUESTION

Explain how it is going with you trying to be in the moment.

Actual student responses (without any corrections)

– *It is quiet relaxing trying to focus on one thing and one thing only. I feel like it takes a lot of stress from your shoulders.*

– *It's going good because I am more focused on what people are saying.*

– *It is going well because I am focusing really well because I stop thinking about other things while I'm on zoom.*

– *It feels good it feels like i'm more interested in the subject.*

– *I'm trying it on my family and it seems like they pay atencion a lot.*

MY INSIGHTS

I am incredibly impressed with their insights and willingness to share with me. We are starting to have a stronger connection. Having students notice that they are in the moment has really helped them be much less stressed. I did not realize that this line of questioning would make students more interested in the subject, allow students to feel like their parents are paying more attention to them, and notably have fewer distractions. We are only touching the surface of the benefits from my students noticing and sharing their feelings / insights.

September 10, 2020 (Week 6 of School – Distance Learning)

QUESTION

What would happen if you make a lot of mistakes?

Actual student responses (without any corrections)

– *you would getin trouble* (many said this)

– *You will learn from them.*

– *If it was a job we could get fired*

– *If I made a lot of mistakes I would probably get worse grades.*

– *I would ask for help and if i made a lot I would try to see how to complete it*

MY INSIGHTS

I was surprised to see that so many students think that they would get into trouble if they made mistakes. We even had a discussion about how many students believed that exact same thing. I want the students to realize that they are not alone in their thinking and feelings. This was a huge realization for me. I never knew that so many students did not want to share a math answer (in the Chat feature of Zoom) because they were afraid that they would get in trouble if their answer could be wrong. We also contrasted making mistakes with making the wrong choices. This meaningful conversation really improved participation. I could tell that they really understood it. After this short discussion, the students started answering more in the chat. They still made mistakes, but they were much more comfortable with it.

September 11, 2020 (Week 6 of School – Distance Learning)

I asked the students how they were feeling. A majority of them said, "Tired and more tired than usual." The students were off today so I wanted to get their mind on something different. They were not yet born when 9/11 happened, so I am not sure why they were not themselves. So, out of nowhere, I thought it was time for a topic change. I told them that I really like french fries dipped in hot fudge.

QUESTION
Share the weirdest food that you have ever tried.
Actual student responses (without any corrections)
– *Hot pepper with cheese*
– *bacon with chocolate*
– *Pizza and Ketchup*
– *I had cheese on hot cheetos*
– *pickles in popcorn with sport pepper*
– *Gummy Bears and syrup*

MY INSIGHTS

I wanted to jolt them out of their funk. This was a spur-of-the-moment discussion to get them to share a little bit more about themselves in a fun and strange way. It worked because they felt comfortable sharing their strange food. I felt like the students were "back to normal."

September 14, 2020 (Week 7 of School – Distance Learning)

QUESTION

Why do you think students are stressed right now?

Actual student responses (without any corrections)

– *some of us are stressed because we are stuck at home.*

– *Because they feel rushed*

– *Students are stressed because they feel overwhelmed with all the work*

– *because my favorite cousin died yesterday* [Me: I am so sorry. How
  are you?] *I am sad.* [Me: If you need to cry, please turn off your
  video and let the tears fall.] He turned off his video and cried.
  My heart broke for him.

MY INSIGHTS

If I had not been asking the students these questions, this young man would never have felt comfortable sharing the information about his cousin with me. That student would have bottled up those feelings for who knows how long. We have spoken several times after that. I can tell that he does not feel alone. These are meaningful connections! We won't know what is going on with students unless we ask them and then listen!

QUESTION

Why don't I accept late homework?

Actual student responses (without any corrections)

– *I think it's so the students don't get overwhelmed with work they
  have to finish.*

— I think that you don't accept late work because you dont want them to stress about finishing it another day
— You don't accept it because doing late work can be stressful.

MY INSIGHTS

I was amazed at their insights because I never thought that they, as students, even thought about my late policy. I do not accept late work because it is stressful for students and for myself. It is not to punish them; it is to make their life easier. Once I explained that to them, they were okay with it.

QUESTION
Do you have a habit of postponing things?
Actual student responses (without any corrections)

— no
— What does postponing mean
— I don't think I do
— Yes because I think I can do it later when that is not true.

MY INSIGHTS

I wanted them to start noticing if they postpone their homework assignments. They are not to judge it, only to notice it.

HOMEWORK
Notice when you postpone things. Just notice.

I sometimes give homework assignments that we do not discuss the next day because they need extra time to notice and process. I will mention the topic of postponing a few times during the next month, then I will wait for the question to come back to my brain, and then we will discuss. Again, I do not force any questions.

September 15, 2020 (Week 7 of School – Distance Learning)

QUESTION

Have you noticed how much help you still need in school?

Actual student responses (without any corrections)

– *no*

– *Yes, I still need a lot of help to be faster*

– *yes*

MY INSIGHTS

During distance learning, students are expected to do so much without a teacher (and some with very little parent support). One day they had help and the next day they were on a computer. It was a stressful situation for everyone. This conversation gave them the opportunity to notice that they still need help, and that it is okay. Everyone needs help; we need only to learn to ask. They felt heard and relieved! They never noticed how uncomfortable they really were.

QUESTION

Have you noticed how much more independent you NEED to be?

Actual student responses (without any corrections)

– *It makes me fell a little grown.*

– *yes and it makes me feel weird*

– *It makes me fell like I have more responsibilities*

– *I have I am a bit nervous because I will have more responsibilities*

MY INSIGHTS

Again, students were thrown into the deep end with distance learning and were expected to be independent right away. They did not know the origins of such discomfort or what it really was until we started to talk about it. They knew they felt "weird," but they could not pinpoint why. They felt much better once we talked. It is all about feeling listened to and included, not isolated and ignored.

QUESTION

Do you feel like you are too young to have all of this responsibility put on you?

Actual student responses (without any corrections)

– *Yes, because it's too much*

– *I think it is because I am not used to being independent*

– *In my opinion no beaue I think it will be great practice for when we're grown up and worried about bills.*

– *yes and no because we get more stressed more easely*

MY INSIGHTS

Wow! My students are only twelve years old and I never thought about asking them how they felt about this sudden feeling of needing to be responsible. We are asking them to do things that are challenging and confusing to them. Again, these conversations are not about trying to fix their problems but, rather, about having students share their feelings so they understand that they never have to say they "shouldn't feel that way".

September 16, 2020 (Week 7 of School – Distance Learning)

MY INSIGHTS

You may be wondering what to say after you ask a question. I am here to reassure you that you do not need to stress! You just need to say what you feel in your heart. Listen to your students and say what comes to you naturally. Your students will know that you care. Sometimes there will be lots of questions and not much teaching, like today for me.

QUESTION

What can teachers/parents do to help YOU be more comfortable with being more responsible?

Actual student responses (without any corrections)

– *Keep supporting and encouraging me.*

– You can me believe in me
– They should show us an example of a situation where you need to be a responsible
– They can help me when I need it and to encourage by saying that thing like mistakes are normal and also being patient but firm and consistent.

MY INSIGHTS

"Responsible" is a commonly used word. I assumed that my students knew what it meant when one said to be responsible. I was wrong. Even correcting these misconceptions helps me connect more deeply with all of my students. Simply by asking questions such as "Hmmm. . . . What does it really mean to be responsible?" Just as it is okay for students to struggle, teachers can too. I had a hard time putting into words what I really wanted to ask, so I thought about it, then again asked the students what they thought.

QUESTION
How can teachers be encouraging to you?
Actual student responses (without any corrections)
– They can keep reminding us that mistakes are okay.
– They can be encouraging to me by telling me i can do it
– Teachers can be encouraging by telling us that we can do it and that we got this
– By telling us compliments on what we did.
– They can explain how responsibility will be important from now on and encourage us to be more responsible

MY INSIGHTS
I asked this question about their need of encouragement to see what their perspective was. I had a gut feeling that it would be different than what I thought. I did not realize that students really

liked compliments and encouragement. I honestly believed that it embarrassed them to receive praise in front of others. A sign that I am still learning.

QUESTION

Do you have teachers that say encouraging things?
Do you have teachers who DO NOT say encouraging things to you?
Actual student responses (without any corrections)

– *I have a few teachers that do have encouraged me and a few who don't.*
– *I have some teachers that say encouraging things and that helps me to work harder*
– *i do i just don't think that that really helps me or that have an effect. i don't know why but when they tell me i can't do it i want to show then i can*

MY INSIGHTS

I found this question particularly interesting because not all of my students answered. I think some students were not comfortable with calling teachers out. Some might have seen it as disrespectful. Reflecting on this question, I could have followed up by also asking them, "Do you ever encourage others?" If they can assess whether they do or don't, then it can make them more aware and conscious of others and their feelings. It is about all levels of connection. For example, the teacher connects with their students. Students connect to themselves and to others.

QUESTION

What can teachers/parents do to help you be more comfortable with being more responsible?
Actual student responses (without any corrections)

– *Believe in me*

– Maybe they can explain to us why we have to be more responsible so that we can understand.
– Teaching us how to be responsible and independent.
– Teachers/Parents can help me be more comfortable with being more responsible and independent by trusting us.

MY INSIGHTS

It broke my heart a little to hear my student say, "Believe in me." I also realized that they do not really know what it means to be responsible. As teachers, we often take on many roles, like being a parent figure, guidance counselor, and role models for our students. So I felt it was my job to discuss – by asking questions – how one can be responsible.

QUESTION

What does it mean for you to be responsible?
Actual student responses (without any corrections)
– To me it means that I have to help in the house or be careful.
– it means to make the right choces
– We have to do out own thin things and behaive
– To me it means to keep track of your own stuff and not have someone reminding you.
– How I understand is to be more careful
– To be responsible means to follow direction, listen, and to remember things yourself.

MY INSIGHTS

The definitions of being responsible vary tremendously along with the level of understanding of that character trait. Many students did not fully understand what it meant to be responsible, but were able to provide examples. This highlighted the importance of continuing to discuss this later.

QUESTION
How do you see teachers being responsible?
Actual student responses (without any corrections)

– *They know what to do every time and they have all the things they need for the class and they dont get distracted.*
– *By teaching us the subject we are doing once or more so we can understand what you are teaching us.*
– *They are responsible by always give us the assignment on time and are always there to help us. Also keeping there word.*
– *I see teachers being responsible by preparing lessons for us.*
– *I see teachers being responsible by letting us in on time. Checking our work and being there to help us.*

MY INSIGHTS
Very interesting. Students were able to explain responsibility as it pertains to their teachers, but they were unable to transfer it to themselves as easily.

QUESTION
Tell me something that you can smile at.
Actual student responses (without any corrections)

– *I'm alive and well*
– *I have a friend whos funny and makes me smile*
– *I can smile at animals such as dogs and cats*
– *I have something to eat everyday and somewhere to sleep at.*
– *Something that I can smile at is just to make my teacher happy or remember a funny memorie.*
– *I smile when people smile at me*

MY INSIGHTS
I wanted them to notice that there are things going on now that make them smile. Not everything is negative and challenging. I wanted to end the day on a happy note. Many students ended up smiling.

September 17, 2020 (Week 7 of School – Distance Learning)

QUESTION
What chores do you have to do?
Actual student responses (without any corrections)
– *I do not have to do chores.*
– *I have to wash the dishes sometimes*
– *I have to take out the trash do the laundry*
– *I have to wash the dishes, sweep the floor, and wash clothes.*
– *Sweep, put the clothes to wash, take the clothes out of the dryer,
   fold the clothes put it away, put clothes to dry, clean the bathroom.*

MY INSIGHTS
In order to see their responsibilities at home, as members of their respective families, I asked them about what chores they had to do. Students inevitably provided me with examples of being responsible in terms that they would understand.

HOMEWORK
Do a chore before your parents ask you to do it. Notice their reaction.

September 23, 2020 (Week 8 of School – Distance Learning)

QUESTION
Did you do a chore before your parents asked you to do it? If so,
what was their reaction?
Actual student responses (without any corrections)
– *Yes,because living in a mexican household is different.There
   reaction was surprised because they always have to tell me.*
– *Yes there reaction was surprised because I spilled a liquid and they
   saw it but I mopped it before they asked and they looked proud*
– *I washed the dishes and my mom was asking me if I was ok*

because I never do anything like that and they where happy.
– *To sweep and I already did it and they were really shocked.*
– *They showed no reaction when I cleaned my room.*
– *I have done a chore before my parents asked me to do it. My mom just told me to go do another chore.*
– *Yes i always do chores everyday like yesterday I washed all dishes and cleaned the table before my parents come home but they never like nothing so they just got very mad and made me and my siblings clean again.*

MY INSIGHTS

The outcome was that if students are excited, then they are more willing to share. I am seeing their confidence grow. I wanted the students to notice that their actions have consequences and it can be a really positive thing.

The negative reactions from the parents in the last few comments led to the discussion that parents are not connected yet. I want the students to notice that right now, their parents are disconnected and it is okay. We will not judge them, but we will kindly and gently teach them the way to connect, even as we grow in our ability to connect.

September 21, 2020 (Week 8 of School – Distance Learning)

QUESTION

How do you feel about the first quarter and your grades?
Actual student responses (without any corrections)
– *I feel bad because they're pretty low*
– *I feel like it been a pretty bumpy ride. Because at the beginning of the quarter my grades weren't the best but now they are much better. SO I would s-ay that I feel pretty proud of myself for getting my grades up.*

– *I feel proud of my self because I can do this and ama never give up and I tried my best to have them good to show them to my parents*

– *I feel worried I have very poor grades the classes are math, science, and history.*

– *I feel bad because I used to have good grade in last year*

MY INSIGHTS

Do teachers ask students how they feel about their grades? If so, do we listen to how they feel? These thoughts are coming from a place of compassion, In no way, shape, or form are we to judge other teachers. These reflections are just to make us all aware that we need to ask the questions and listen to what the students say. We may often think that students do not care about their grades, but after reading their thoughts, I know that they do.

QUESTION

Tell me something you are proud of from this quarter.

Actual student responses (without any corrections)

– *I am proud of raising my grades because I had mostly F's.*

– *I am proud of making this far in the school year.*

– *This quarter I am proud of how far I have gone since today and even though I did give up at one point,I kept going with my life and school.*

– *There isn't space.* (This one made me smile.)

MY INSIGHTS

Teachers need to have students see the positive side of things. There are a lot of positive things even when we do not notice them. The students also need to notice that there are things that they do that they should be proud of. This type of awareness and consciousness needs to be practiced so that it becomes very natural. This goes for students and teachers, too.

QUESTION
What do I mean, "Don't be so hard on yourself?"
Actual student responses (without any corrections)
– *I think for me it means Don't doubt yourself or overthink it*
– *To not beat myself up when I fail at something or I make a mistake.*
– *I think it means to don't be mean to me self*
– *I think it means that I shouldn't be hard and mean on myself and think I can't do things.*
– *I think that means I don't have to get mad at myself because I am trying my best.*

MY INSIGHTS
Having students notice how they are feeling – and articulating those sentiments – is life-changing. This awareness allows them to connect with how they feel and to dissolve any feeling of alienation.

HOMEWORK
Catch if your say something negative about yourself. Catch one time at least that you say something unkind to yourself.

QUESTION
What do you say to yourself? Negative stuff?
Actual student responses (without any corrections)
– I'm dumb.
– *I'm not smart enough for this.*
– *I tell myself that I'm dumb, stupid, not good enough, useless.*
– *I'm not smart why a'm i like this and i wish i was better.*
– *I say that I am bad at the stuff i do*
– *I say " why can't I get this correct it's so easy but Im just not smart"*

MY INSIGHTS

Students need to be provided with opportunities to feel heard. This is how they can share their true feelings. If they can catch these thoughts, then they can stop this negativity from spreading. I explained to the students that it is like a little child getting ready to sneak a cookie, because when the mom sees the child, the child stops. It is the same with their thoughts and emotions. Notice them, and you can stop them. Don't notice them, and they can continue.

HOMEWORK:

Did you catch a time where you were hard on yourself?

September 22, 2020 (Week 8 of School – Distance Learning)

QUESTION

Did you catch a time when you were hard on yourself?
Actual student responses (without any corrections)

– Yes, yesterday I struggled with an assignments on khan and I said am never going to finish.
– A time I was hard on my self yesterday was when I was painting I told myself that I can't do it.
– Yes I caught a time where I was being hard on myself while doing other classwork because I was slow.
– Yes, I felt disappointed of myself because I forgot to do my chores but I did them later on.
– Yes because yesterday while I was doing khan I told myself I can't do it and caught it.

MY INSIGHTS

I read many of the comments aloud without saying names so they could hear that they had very similar comments. This question allowed students to catch their thoughts, become aware and, with that sense of consciousness, release the strong hold that feeling had on them. Letting themselves know they are not alone in their feelings.

QUESTION

How do you feel about making mistakes?

Actual student responses (without any corrections)

– *I feel nervous of making mistakes*

– *I feel ashamed of myself.*

– *I feel like I'm letting myself down.*

– *i feel nervous and scared*

– *I feel annoyed about making a mistake.*

MY INSIGHTS:

To be honest, I did not realize that they felt this way. Students are noticing and sharing their fears. I told them this was a sign that they are starting to realize what is holding them back from learning, paying attention, and being successful. Having those strong emotions and anxieties about making mistakes. My advice was to notice the feeling. Information is power! This information will help me, as a teacher, be more compassionate and understanding.

MEDITATION

Today, we sat still for one minute with our eyes closed and listened.

This helps them to notice what is going on around them. I asked them what they heard.

Actual student responses (without any corrections)

– *Nothing*

– *I heard my fish tank and the cars*

– *In my head I heard like a voice saying keep trying, keep fighting you will make it* (this is not what I meant but it's a start)

– *I heard the tree leaves moving and shacking*

– *birds,phone,car drive by*

MY INSIGHTS

Students need to be taught how to listen and be aware, which comes from practice. It only takes one minute of being still and listening. This tiny meditation also calms them tremendously.

HOMEWORK

Catch a time that you feel icky because you made a mistake.

Exercise
I want to thank myself for....
Actual student responses (without any corrections)

– *I want to thank myself for being a good listener.*
– *I want to thank myself for learning how to simplify correctly when multiplying fractions.*
– *I want to thank myself for learning a trick to find LCM*
– *I want to thank myself for learning how to multiply fractions today.*

MY INSIGHTS

We are our own worst critics. Students are no exception. Students are so hard on themselves. Students very rarely say something kind to themselves, let alone others. Today may have been the first time that they were able to pause, notice, and thank themselves for something "good" that they did.

September 23, 2020 (Week 8 of School – Distance Learning)

QUESTION

What is holding you back from paying attention and participating in class?
Actual student responses (without any corrections:

– *Well for me personally I get distracted pretty easy but I think I've gotten better at paying attention more in class. And sometimes I*

don't want to participate because I'm afraid I'll get judged if I get a wrong answer.
– *What is holding me back is having the urge to use my phone during class and not doing all the work.*
– *The thing that might be holding me back is by day-dreaming about 5 minutes ago I was thinking about something else and I caught it and stopped it.*
– *Things that are holding me back are family problems.*
– *There is a lot of things around me that make noise or distract me*

MY INSIGHTS

I noticed that my students are noticing and verbalizing what is holding them back. The whole purpose is for the students to just notice how they are without judging. They are taking their first steps towards having compassion for themselves.

September 24, 2020 (Week 8 of School – Distance Learning)

QUESTION
What really interests you? What are you curious about?
Actual student responses (without any corrections)
– *What really interest me is outer space because of my dads history channels.*
– *I'm curious about what people think when they are silent.*
– *What am curious about is how deep is the ocean.*
– *Something that interests me is the thought of how the first humans on earth were made.*
– *I am curious about if everything in the future would be very different like robots as workers*
– *I was washing the dishes I and than I wondered why do my fingers get wrinkly*
– *I am curious about space are we the only ones in space are we to late or early.*

– what I'm curious about is our sleep we have been doing it for years but why do we need it

– I'm interested in how chemist make new chemicals and how they do it.

MY INSIGHTS

I wanted the students to share a little bit about themselves. It was another chance to connect with them and for them to feel the connection strengthening. They are more likely to share with questions of their interests, and I can tell they are starting to participate more.

September 25, 2020 (Week 8 of School – Distance Learning)

QUESTION

Do you ever feel like you don't belong? Explain and be as honest as you can, please.

Actual student responses (without any corrections)

– yes because people don't pay attention to me

– I'm not sure I can find the words for it.

– Sometimes when I see others differently I feel like I don't belong and I try to be like them by doing similar stuff that they do.

– I do fell like I don;t belong because in luch I flt like no one cared Id I sat with them or not.

– It's not that I think I don't belong it's just that sometimes I feel like I have to fit in because I'm really scared of getting judged by people.

– will sometimes I feel like I belong somewhere else a place that people don't judge me be who I a'm

– Yes, I have a lot because when I'm around my family I feel like I don't belong because I don't always meet my families expectaions

– I have never felt this way but if I did I will have always have support- ive parents that explain if things are normal and that help me.

– Yes, for a long time I felt like I didn't belong because I didn't know

any english my first language is spanish and didn't understand anybody.
– *Sometimes with my family to at parties I see them all laughing and having fun but I'm an introvert and I feel like I don't belong.*
– *I have sometimes felt like I don't belong because I feel like people would be better of without me and I sometimes think about it over and over about it at (I spoke with this student and found out he is already in counseling)*

MY INSIGHTS

I shared a lot of student examples with you to show the depth of their pain. Reading their shares in the chat broke my heart. There were times I was trying to hold back my tears, but I did not. Adults have feelings, too. I try to read a lot of them out loud because that only reiterates their sense of belonging.

I told them that I felt their pain because it was how I felt when I was younger, but no one told me that it was okay to feel these ways. I told them that they always have a place where they belong because they are here. I reminded them that their feelings are perfect and notice them. We meditated right after this discussion so that they could really notice their feelings and dissolve their hurt. Remember, there are always alternatives to meditation. If your school does not allow you to meditate, then maybe you could just have them breathe deeply for three times with their eyes open.

QUESTION

You have been meditating for 8 weeks now. How has it helped you?
Be specific.
Actual student responses (without any corrections)
– *I has helped me be more calm and brethe more deeply.*
– *It helped me from being angry*
– *It has helped me be more relaxed and not be worried about things.*

– It has helped me feel relaxed instead of stressed.
– Meditating has helped me be less stressed about school work and it has helped
– It helped by helping me getting rid of other feelings so I could of get in the moment at the right time.
– It has helped me with expressing my emotions and letting all my negative thoughts flow away.
– It has helped me stay calm and not be hard on myself like I was last year it helped me to not worry.

MY INSIGHTS

Meditating for only three minutes a day has helped my students tremendously. Students are now able to notice and explain how they feel. They are starting to connect to themselves and it will help them to connect with others. They are also starting to learn about compassion. I wish I had learned to meditate when I was younger since it is a great awareness strategy and healing mechanism.

ℒ

This is the end of the first quarter of school. I will continue to flow with whatever questions come to me during class for the second quarter. It will be exciting to see how it unfolds throughout the year and how much deeper the connection gets between the students, themselves, and others. I am also looking forward to seeing how the students' stress levels continue to go down, how much more confident they become, and how they will continue to grow in their self-awareness.

Please remember that this journey will need to be nurtured, and it may not be quick and easy with all students. Do not beat yourself up if you cannot easily connect with certain students. Keep questioning and listening to see what unfolds.

QUARTER TWO

Seventh-grade students' unedited comments after about 15 weeks of questions, shares, and listening

– *I also forgot to say thank you for letting us share are feelings and thoughts it helps when we are really down so thank you:*

– *Goodbye have an amazing day and weekend stay safe and have fun also thank you for teaching us these things and letting us feel comfterable when we share some things.*

– *thank you for letting us trust you to share out feelings*

– *I feel better talking about how I feel because now I feel like at least someone cares*

– *It bothers me how fast you managed to get me to open up to you about my emotions because usually I don't open about my emotion for example my best friend I've known her for almost 4 years and I'm barely opening up to her on my feelings and emotions.*

October 14, 2020 (Week 9 of School – Distance Learning)

QUESTION
What do you think you messed up on during the first quarter?
Be specific.
Actual student responses (without any corrections)

– *I think I messed up on turning in late work by working on another subject.*

– *I have a lot of missing assingments*

– *I think I mest up on everything I was doing bad in my test and my homework I mest up on*

– *I think I messed up on fully being in the moment because their are very little things that could distract me but because we are learning it slowly goes away.*

MY INSIGHTS

For students to fix a problem, they have to first notice what it is. If they do not even recognize it, they cannot fix it. It was nice to see how honest and willing they were to share what they messed up on WITHOUT judging it.

There will be days where we go through a series of questions that unfold during our discussions. Some days, there is a lot of talking and connecting, and a little bit of teaching. Right now, it is important that the students feel connected. After the connection is made and strong, teaching and learning will become much easier. Right now, teaching is a challenge and so is their learning.

QUESTION

What can you promise yourself that you will TRY in order to raise your grade?

Actual student responses (without any corrections)

– *I can promise that I will do all the work needed on time,attend zoom every day,do what I am asked for.*

– *something I promise to myself to try to do is being more careful with tests and always participate*

– *I will promise to myself That I will do my work and turn it in on time.*

– *try to do all my assingest and i will try to show up to all classes*

– *I want to try not give up on myself by saying that I can't do something.*

MY INSIGHTS

I asked this question so that the students could begin to notice their "problem." If they are not even aware that there is an issue, they will not be able to change it. Being aware is incredibly important, a skill that we will continue to practice.

I was impressed that the students wanted me to know that they really want to succeed in school. I feel like the students are beginning to feel more comfortable sharing with me.

QUESTION

Starting today, what are your "work hours?"

Actual student responses (without any corrections)

– *mine re by 7:30 to 1:00*

– *8:00-3:15*

– *7:30-5:00pm*

MY INSIGHTS

Since the students' main issue is not turning in stuff on time, I wanted them to see distance learning as their job. I shared that my work hours are 7:30 to 4:00 and at 4:00, I am done. I do not do any school stuff after 4:00.

If they can see a fixed end time, they will finish more work before their day ends. The students will feel less stressed because they will start learning to manage their time better.

QUESTION

What did you do that was a little interesting over the break?

Actual student responses (without any corrections)

– *I experienced a very painful fall of a bike.*

– *I had a movie nigh with my family wich was pretty nice because we dont do that often and it was wired at first but got used it*

– *Got surgery*

– Something interesting I did over the break was visit my cousins grave yard but then I get left at the gas station when we were going back home.

MY INSIGHTS

I am sorry to admit that I had a very hard time controlling my laughter at the student being left at the gas station. I think it was so funny because it was so "wrong." (which is not a judgment). I knew she was ok because she was in class.

This opened up a huge discussion and an incredible chance to connect even more with the students outside of any academics. I apologized to the students for laughing, though they were smiling, too. The student who got left behind was also smiling. I noticed that she felt very important in this conversation because she used to feel invisible.

Also, here is another chance for me to connect with the student who fell off a bike and the one who had surgery. They have opened up to me and now, it is my turn to reach out and talk to them.

Remember, these questions are not scripted and they happen organically. I could not have made up the following question if the students had not shared their experiences with me.

QUESTION

Have you ever been left before?

Actual student responses (without any corrections)

– when I was small i got forgotten at the store and i was crying

– Well my parents left me at Costco.

– One time we went to a water park and they left me there and I was really scared because i was like 8 or 9 years old and and they had left me there for like an 1 hour or 2

– Yes my dad forgot me at the mall when I was six.

MY INSIGHTS

I was surprised at how many students shared that they had been left somewhere before. Here was another chance for the students to share their feelings and to be heard. This was a really scary time in their life, which may still be affecting them now. Many realized that they were not alone in this scenario because other parents have forgotten their children before. This topic led me to another question.

QUESTION

Do you know why your parents did that?
Actual student responses (without any corrections)
– *they were not in the moment and were probably stersted.*
– *They got to distracted*
– *Talking to friends*
– *i think that they had a lot of things in mind and weren't in the moment*

MY INSIGHTS

I do NOT have any judgment here at all. I wanted the student to start thinking about what could happen if they are not in the present moment. Parents and adults are very stressed, disconnected, and often not present mentally. They do not even realize that they are so distracted. It's no one's fault.

We need to realize that the parents, too, are struggling now. Parents have been thrown into teaching while still having to work and take care of everything. Parents are stressed and I am hoping that by having the students share, connect, feel ok, and meditate, it will also help the parents. If the students are calm, it is one less stressor for parents.

I shared that meditating and noticing their emotions will help them tremendously to become present and aware (so that they do not leave their children somewhere when they are older).

43

October 15, 2020 (Week 9 of School – Distance Learning)

QUESTION

Were you able to finish all of your work during your work hours? How did it feel?

Actual student responses (without any corrections)

– *yes because it was easy and I felt proud of myself*
– *no because I had a lot of work to do and the homework and*
  I feel worried.
– *no it didn't because I still procrastinate*
– *I stuck with my work hours I even finished before. I felt accomplished.*

MY INSIGHTS

Many students were so proud of themselves and many were still feeling stressed. I had some of them modify their work hours to help with the stress. I told them that work hours would help them have an end time so that the whole day is not just stressing about schoolwork. I asked them to notice how often they say "later" so that they can become aware of how much they procrastinate. It is about being aware and not being hard on themselves.

October 19, 2020 (Week 10 of School – Distance Learning)

QUESTION

What did you hear? [We had done a listening meditation for one minute. Eyes closed, sitting still and listening.]

Actual student responses (without any corrections)

– *I heard some birds singing and my dog playing in the leaves.*
– *I didn't hear anything because of how calm I was.*
– *I felt more calm because I did't hear anything it felt pacful.*
– *I heard birds and cars and a fan*

MY INSIGHTS

Students are not used to just listening and paying attention to what they hear. Many students said that they hear "nothing" and it is because they have not learned to be fully present and simply listen yet. Their minds are going a mile a minute and this meditation helps it calm down. We will continue to practice the listening meditation and see how their listening evolves.

October 20, 2020 (Week 10 of School – Distance Learning)

QUESTION
How do you feel right now?
Actual student responses (without any corrections)
– *I feel nervous about my meet with my parents*
– *Because a lot happened yesterday at home and I don't know how to feel about it*
– *Exited for the day because I finished my work hours earlier yesterday and hope to do the same today*

One-on-one conversations
Student 1: *I feel dizzy because I feel like Im not doing things right*
Me: I told her to feel exactly how she feels. It's perfect. Don't change it, just notice it. I saw the relief on her face.

Student 2 – I feel angry because i don't like to wake up early.
Me: I told her that I felt the same way when I was younger. I said that I hoped she could find a job where she was able to sleep in. She smiled.

At times, I talk directly to the child without revealing what they said to the class and it is magical to see how they feel validated and heard. Taking a couple of minutes helps create a stronger connection between the teacher and the student.

MY INSIGHTS

I noticed at the beginning of class that the students did not seem like their normal selves so, I asked them how they were feeling. Many of them said, "Stressed, nervous, and anxious." I had them explain what was going on. Many were worried about parent conferences and some had issues going on at home. After they "felt heard," I noticed they were calm and I was able to start teaching.

Their attendance on Zoom has gone way up since the beginning of the year, and I know it is because of how connected we are now. The students feel heard, important, and valued! I am really enjoying teaching on Zoom much more than before. I also have very little stress and I am sleeping better than I have in years! What a great by-product of connecting with students.

It is simply about asking them questions and listening to their answers.

QUESTION

Why are you so uncomfortable with parent conferences?

Actual student responses (without any corrections)

– *I feel a little nervous since my ILP (conference) is today.*

– *nervous*

– *nervous*

– *nervous*

– *nervous*

– *nervous*

– *nervous*

– *I feel disappointed.*

Actual dialogue between a student and me during this sharing
Student: I feel dizzy because I feel like Im not doing things right
Me: Try to just be in the moment. Only focus on what is in front of you right now. That will help you a lot.

Student: I try but i just feel dizzy and I keep shaking and Im just trying to calm down my anxiety"

We did the Serene Mind Meditation and this was her share: *I cried a little; i cried a little because I felt like birds and angels were bringing me with my cousin who passed away.*

Me: Feel what you feel and don't try to change it. Whatever emotion that comes up is perfect. Let it out and know that it's OK.

Serene Mind Meditation

I have done this meditation many times for myself and have become an expert before I did it with students. I lead it myself with kid-friendly language instead of having them listen to it.

Preethaji (2018). Serene Mind. Retrieved from https://www.youtube.com/watch?v=OXg8xcWBMuo.

MY INSIGHTS

"Nervous, nervous, nervous" was the theme for today because of parent conferences. I did not realize that so many students felt the same way but I knew they felt better hearing that others were feeling exactly like them. They felt connected and not alone.

Today, even though I was mostly talking to one student about focusing on what is going on now, what I was saying to her applied to the whole class. All teachers need to talk to their students. Some teachers do not want to know what is going on, but this is NOT about the teacher. This is about helping students who do not have someone to talk to (or do not feel like they can) and who don't know that what they are feeling is ok. Letting students know that what they are feeling is normal and that others feel the same way is incredibly important in connecting deeply with students. So many students felt alone, but once they heard that someone else was going through the same issue, they felt much better.

QUESTION

How do you think teachers feel about parent conferences?
Actual student responses (without any corrections)
– *they feel super nervous to talk to the parents*
– *I think they feel the same as students just not scared of getting in trouble because they don't have to worry about it because it's not their parents.*
– *I feel like they take a few deep breaths and get calm*

MY INSIGHTS

I am impressed that they are starting to feel empathy. They are realizing that teachers are humans also, with the same feelings as them. They are becoming aware that we are more alike than different and this is huge at such an early age.

October 21, 2020 (Week 10 of School – Distance Learning)

Conversation: The student who was struggling yesterday showed up to Zoom (she misses a lot of class) and I said, "I'M SO HAPPY TO SEE YOU TODAY!!!" She said, 'Hiii im trying to make my mom proud." I said, "How about making yourself proud, too?" She smiled.

MY INSIGHTS

This student missed the next three days of class. Many times, there are circumstances beyond a teacher's control, and the connection is a work in progress. Do not be discouraged. Keep asking questions and listening to their responses. This connection will not happen overnight, so be patient with how quickly or slowly it is unfolding.

QUESTION

How did the breakout rooms feel? In Zoom, I can put the students in separate rooms of two or three students where they can talk and do work.

Actual student responses (without any corrections)

– *shy*

– *weird*

– *nervous*

– *Uncomftorable*

– *super awkward*

MY INSIGHTS

This is why I ask questions even though I think I know the answer. I was wrong again in my assumption that they would talk in a breakout room. I had NO idea that they would feel so uncomfortable. I was pleasantly surprised that they were able to verbalize how they felt. At the beginning of the year, I would only get "good" or "bad". They are really growing in noticing their feelings. We will continue in breakout rooms until they dissolve their feelings of discomfort.

I was an incredibly shy student and I wish I had someone to push me out of my comfort zone and speak. I had a lot to say but was terrified to share. I hope that, in time, by using the breakout rooms, the students will notice their emotions and heal their fear.

QUESTION

Did you notice how you felt while in the breakout room?

Actual student responses (without any corrections)

– *I felt that I was confident and I did catch it*

– *yes*

– *no*

MY INSIGHTS

I want the students to "catch" their feelings at the time it is happening. If they can notice it at that moment, really feel it, not judge it, it may dissolve.

Many students and adults rarely even notice their emotions, let alone feel them fully. No one has taught them to do so. Most people ignore what they're feeling in hopes that they will go away. In reality, these emotions get stronger if they are ignored. I am so happy that my students are learning this now, not when they are fifty-plus years old.

October 22, 2020 (Week 10 of School – Distance Learning)
QUESTION
Did you catch it when you felt uncomfortable in the breakout room?
Actual student responses (without any corrections)
– *No and I was scared*
– *Yes*
– *Yes*
– *Yes*
– *Yes*
– *Yes I did catch it then it just poofed away.*

MY INSIGHTS
Noticing one's emotions is a process and the students are doing it! About 90% said, "Yes." I loved the comment from the student who said, *"Yes I did catch it then it just poofed away."* She now has "proof" that catching the emotion makes it dissolve. Dissolving stressful emotions is very quick for younger people, but it may take a few tries for people who are older and that is ok.

QUESTION
Tell me something that makes you smile.
Actual student responses (without any corrections)
– *one thing that makes me smile is going to the cemetery to see my grandma.*
– *food*

– *One thing that makes me smile is my dog*
– *One thing that makes me happy is that I made mistakes and fixed them and grew from them.*

MY INSIGHTS

I wanted to ask a fun question to get them to smile. It also gave me a little insight into what makes them happy.

QUESTION

Share something from the meditation. [Serene Mind]
Actual student responses (without any corrections)
– *This meditation helped me wake up because I saw everything cearer* (clearer)
– *My brain got lost in the moment*
– *Something about this meditation that I found cool was that my emotions went from happy to calm and all of a sudden I felt more relaxed.*
– *I was really in the moment and avoided all my thoughts.*

MY INSIGHTS

Meditation is helping the students at a very deep level. They are able to notice that it makes them calm, relaxed, and in the moment. This is a life-altering journey. Imagine where the students will be when they are 25 years old and able to be calm and in the moment.

October 23, 2020 (Week 10 of School – Distance Learning)

QUESTION

What does it mean to YOU to be in the moment?
Actual student responses (without any corrections)
– *Don't worry about the pas or the future.*
– *To pay attention to what you are doing*

– To me it means that we do what we are doing in the present and not something for the furure

– I think it means that when you be in the moment is to pay attention to the person you are listening or talking to

MY INSIGHTS

Students are starting to recognize that being in the moment means to pay attention to what is going on in front of you right now. This skill will help students tremendously in life with their friends, family, work, etc..

We discussed that many adults are so worried about the future and are very stressed about what is going on right now, that they are missing out on what is happening in front of them.

I had a conference with a parent yesterday and while the child was talking, the parent was not listening, so the child just waited. I could tell the child knew that her mom was not in the moment. Kids are observant, and now they know what it means to be in the present moment.

I am also noticing that most students are paying much closer attention in class because they have learned how to focus when I am teaching, talking, or being silly. They are also starting to catch themselves when they move out of the moment and start daydreaming.

QUESTION

Have you ever noticed when you are daydreaming?

Actual student responses (without any corrections)

– I don't really notice it.

– yes

– no

– Yes, and it's confusing because sometimes it feels real and all of a sudden I'm snapped back to reality.

MY INSIGHTS

I told the class that all they need to do is notice that they are daydreaming and catch it as soon as they can. After you catch the first one, the rest will be much easier to notice, your daydreaming will lessen, and paying attention will be much easier. You will be able to stay in the moment, and learning will become easier. Also, teaching will be easier since the students are paying better attention.

QUESTION

-Do you catch when your mind wanders?
Actual student responses (without any corrections)
– *not really, my daydreamers are unstoppable*
– *I don't think I've ever caught a time I've daydream*
– *I catch it in between*

MY INSIGHTS

I told the student who said that his dreams were unstoppable that it was just a habit for him. It has been a "normal" part of his life but if he wants them to stop, it can happen. He just needs to notice and then it will stop.

I've noticed that since I taught about catching their daydreams, the students can and are doing it, and it is happening less frequently. I see more students fully engaged when I am teaching, and their learning is increasing.

As a child, I never knew that all I needed to do was notice my daydreams for them to disappear. I wish I had had this knowledge.

QUESTION

How do you stay in the present moment?
Actual student responses (without any corrections)
– *By being calm and focused.*
– *By focusing on what's important right now and forget about the past*

– You stay in the moment by not focusing on the future or past just the moment
– I just like to be in conversations and that's how i'm in the moment.

MY INSIGHTS

They are starting to put into practice what I have been teaching. Being in the moment means to not worry about the past or the future and just focus on what is going on right now.

Being in the moment also means that if I am teaching, they listen. If they are doing homework, it is doing homework, not focusing on the work they did not do yesterday. If they are playing video games, it is not worrying about homework. If they are eating pizza, it is not focusing on playing video games. It is listening when their parents are talking, not focusing on what is on TV. I am so impressed that they are learning and living this!

October 27, 2020 (Week 11 of School – Distance Learning)

QUESTION

Write one sentence explaining how talking about how you feel has helped you this year. How did you feel at the beginning of the year and how do you feel now?

Actual student responses (without any corrections)

– i feel like my emonshins were bottle up and I feel the bottle broke
Me: I told this child to become a writer.
– I felt a bit weird talking about my emotions and later on I felt better about sharing my emotions so I feel happy that somebody listens to me.
– I feel better talking about how I feel because now I feel like at least someone cares
– At the beginning of the year I was all like «Umm how am I suppose to explain how I am feeling. Right now in the present day I can explain how I am feeling really good

– I feel like talking about my feelings was kinda weird at the beginning at the year but know I find it normal. It's makes me feel like someone cares for my feelings.

– I feel like talking about how I feel about this year made me feel more socialize when I'm around people because usually I am quiet around people but now that I express my feelings I'm getting better at socializing.

– I feel happy because i am able to express my thoughts and emotions so that i am not a real emotion disaster.

– It has helped me feel more calm because I am noticing my feelings.

– At first I felt stressed but you taught me to notice it and it has gone away so I feel less stressed

– It has helped me by expressing my feelings and I feel good when you ask us because I let I let my feeling's out. In the beginning it was weird but now if feels good.

– I felt very stressed and angry at the beginning of the year and now I feel a lot calmer and more relaxed.

– It has helped me to know that I have someone that cares about my feelings and how I feel, I feel like I have someone that I can express my feelings too now.

– talking about how I feel helps me be aware of my feelings so I can change my behavior if necessary. Ex. if I notice I'm anxious, I can take a minute to breathe or get whatever I'm stressed about doing done. (share from a teacher)

– It helped me because you catch it and its gone. I felt scared and nervous and now I'm comfortable.

– at the beginning I felt weird about telling someone how I feel and now it's normal to me and I've learn how to talk about my feelings in a paragraph and I'm grateful

MY INSIGHTS

I shared a lot of student comments because it was hard to pick only a few. I also wanted to show how they have grown from the beginning of the year, not only in their emotions but in their ability to express them.

These twelve-year-olds have come a long way in about nine weeks. It is all about asking questions and listening to their answers. The students feel heard, less stressed, calm, and important. They are also able to talk about their feelings and have become much more confident with friends and family. They are becoming transformed human beings.

This share came from a male student: *"I feel happy because i am able to express my thoughts and emotions so that i am not a real emotion disaster."* I am incredibly impressed that he can express himself like this and that he is not ashamed or embarrassed. Can you just imagine how he will be as a grown man? I am so proud!

Asking questions and having students answer them is making a huge difference in his life and in the lives of all of these students. I hope that you are starting to feel comfortable in asking your students (or children) questions also.

October 28, 2020 (Week 11 of School – Distance Learning)

QUESTION
How do you relate to the phrase, "NOTHING WILL STOP YOU!"?
Actual student responses (without any corrections)

– *That if we believe nothing will get in our way then NOTHING will get in our way.*
– *yes the pandemic has stopped me a little and I have noticed that and know I am trying way harder to do good in school. And know I feel like nothing can stop me*
– *It relates to me because it's something that I think of when I'm doing work especially throughout this pandemic and it's also very inspiring. My goal is to attend college.*

– Learning because of the pandemic is really hard but if you try your best and have faith in yourself you can do it.

MY INSIGHTS

Students sometimes just need a few words of encouragement like "Nothing is standing in the way of your success!" or "NOTHING WILL STOP YOU!" A motivational talk is just what they needed to hear today to keep their energy and focus on learning and succeeding.

As the students were leaving class today, I had them all write a motivational phrase to themselves in the chat. They wrote things such as "I got this," "nothing is standing in my way," and "nothing will stop me!!!!" I could feel the words when I read them. I think they felt them also.

I just noticed that many of the students are writing their sentences using "you" instead of "I." I will have them start owning their comments by using "I" statements because it has a different feel and I want them to learn that.

QUESTION

While you were in the breakout room, did you catch an emotion?
What was it?
Actual student responses (without any corrections)

– nervous

– awkward

– nervous

– nervous

– awkward

– At first it was embarrassing but then we started talking about sports and then video games and we played the same ones so we started talking more

– I wasn't nervous surprisingly.

57

MY INSIGHTS

I am asking the same question about how they feel in breakout rooms often so that catching the emotions becomes second nature to them. I am noticing that they are learning to catch the emotion and some of them have even dissolved the feeling of being nervous and embarrassed. They still have a ways to go, but they are on the right track.

November 3, 2020 (Week 12 of School – Distance Learning)

QUESTION

How was the breakout room? How did you feel?

Actual conversation with one student (without any corrections)

– I don't know how not to feel nervous

ME: Where did you feel it in your body?

– I feel it in my head because I wanted to talk but its just didn't come out

Me: I TOTALLY UNDERSTAND!!!! That was me all throughout school.

Me: I was able to dissolve the fear of talking and that is what I want for you. Is that what you want also?

– Yeah I do want it so I can talk with new people and make new friend. But its just so hard for me.

Me: We will get it!!

MY INSIGHTS

Since I have been asking questions almost daily, the students are starting to feel more comfortable with opening up and sharing their deep emotions and fears. Students need a way to express what they are feeling and know that others have gone through the same thing.

I am so proud that the young man that I had the one-on-one conversation with felt that he could share this with me. He is a child who is always smiling and seems to be very happy but I know that he is screaming inside. Because of his fearless shares with me, he is beginning to notice – and in time will conquer – his fear of speaking up. I am excited to see how he changes by the end of the school year. He also knows that he is not the only one going through this discomfort.

QUESTION
Tell me about your work hours.
Actual conversation with one student (without any corrections):
– *I get something's done but I sometimes can't get something done when I am doing some other work*
Me: Try to stay in the moment when you do your homework. Only focus on ONE thing at a time and just notice when your mind goes somewhere else.

MY INSIGHTS
Both of these students are struggling but what is incredible is that they are willing to share how they feel and notice their discomfort. One child is nervous and the other is not staying in the present moment. Again, it is all about noticing the emotion that comes up without judging it. They are comfortable sharing their emotions with me AND this is what connection is all about between students and teachers.

I had private chats with both students and then shared with the whole class how difficult it was for me to talk when I was younger. I struggled, but then once I was able to catch the fear and discomfort, it slowly started to go away. I also shared that I am still learning how to stay in the moment because I get distracted. It will take time some time, but we will get it.

To take it a step further, they can notice the sensation in their body. This will help the stressful emotion dissolve even easier and more quickly.

QUESTION

Tell me about your work hours.

Actual student responses (without any corrections)

– *my work hours are working good because I was finsh at least 30 minutes or try before my work hour ends.*

– *Its not really stressing me out.*

– *I don't really feel stressed about my work hours.*

– *I think it's helping by giving me a goal and since I like completing goals, I try finishing my work fast. It don't stress me.*

– *I don't really think it's working and it's not really stressing me.*

MY INSIGHTS

I had a meeting yesterday with my grade-level team and they told me that the students are feeling stressed because of their work hours. Therefore, I decided to ask the students directly and they overwhelmingly said that the work hours are not stressing them out.

I thought about it a bit and realized that the teachers are stressed more than they think they are. I am saying this in the most respectful way possible to all teachers. All teachers are allowed to be stressed and please remember to give yourselves a break. We are all doing the best we know how to do. This also goes for parents.

November 4, 2020 (Week 12 of School – Distance Learning)

QUESTION

How do you really feel right now? Why do you think you feel that way? Please be honest.

Actual student responses (without any corrections):

– *I am feeling scared because of the election of who is going to win.*

– *I feel happy that the year 2020 is almost over.*

– *I feel streets that I have mostly all F and people keep pushing me and I am trying but nothing works. And it just feels like 100 pounds whats are on my shoulders.*

– Right now I feel slightly overwhelmed and stressed because just thinking of all the work from other classes that I need to do.

– I feel calm and like I'm in this moment because I am on focusing on this right now.

– I feel nervous but I'm not sure why.

– I feel happy because my mom paid full attention to me when we talked Me: YEAH!!!

MY INSIGHTS

Again, I am asking the students how they feel, but this time I had them try to figure out why. If they know why they are feeling a certain way, they may be able to change what is making them feel stressed. For example, if a student is stressed because they have a lot of late homework to do, maybe they can learn to not procrastinate and do the work on time.

That being said, at this moment, the focus is on their inner feelings and not why it is happening. If they can truly feel and notice what is going on inside of their body, they can dissolve it instead of run away from it. So often, we indulge in TV, video games, or social media to not feel what emotion is really going on. The emotion is ignored, and it will come back later with more intensity.

The goal is to have these stressful inner feelings dissolve NOW so that they do not follow them to adulthood.

My Meditation Sharing: Past-Present Moment-Future

I told the students that when I meditated yesterday, I had a picture in my mind where I saw future and past thoughts outside of my brain connected to cords. I saw a huge pair of scissors cut the future and past cords because they were not needed. The only thing that was needed in my mind were the thoughts that were happening in the moment. I drew a picture of it for the students and you should have seen their faces because the visual made a lot of sense to them. This will help them stay more in the present moment because now they are starting to understand what I mean by the present moment.

I did not ask for comments, but one student shared her thoughts: *"I thought if she can cut everything that is stressing her, so can I."*

November 6, 2020 (Week 12 of School – Distance Learning)

QUESTION:
Did you catch any future thoughts that annoyed or bothered you?
Actual student responses (without any corrections)
– *I used to think about the future a lot but now I have already learned to cut it off.*
– *I have not caught a future thought that annoys or bothers me.*
– *I have caught a couple of future thoughts but there are some that still stress me.*
– *A future thought I get is « what if I don't finish on time».*
– *Yes I have caught a lot of futer thoughts and some ar that what might happen if trump wins or if biden wins or if something really bad is going to happen if we dont do anything about the pallution.*

MY INSIGHTS

I taught them yesterday about catching their past and future thoughts and I am amazed that a few have already learned to "cut it off". I know that I will have to review this often so it becomes natural for them to do until they can stay focused on what is right in front of them at any given moment.

Because I continue to ask questions, I have realized how many students are so worried about the future. I had no idea. I need to talk about it more so that the students can "cut the thought off."

QUESTION
What do you think is my favorite food?
Actual student responses (without any corrections)
– eggs with chocolate sauce
– Tacos?
– Spaghetti
– berry ice cream

MY INSIGHTS, Especially for Teachers

I wanted to lighten the mood and the question about my favorite food just came to me so I asked them. Please remember to ask questions that come to you and that are not forced because the students will notice that it feels weird because it does not flow naturally and easily.

Last week I wrote down questions before class and tried to ask the same questions to everyone and it was a complete failure. I did not like it and they were not interested and didn't share very much.

I have three classes and I have realized that it is ok to ask different questions depending on what comes to my mind at the time. Sometimes, I am in the middle of teaching integers, a question comes to me, and I gently stop to ask. It is about naturally connecting, and it will happen when it is supposed to. Maybe at the beginning, have a couple of questions ready, but then let them flow.

If the questions do not come naturally, notice how you are feeling during class. Are you stressed, unsure, or uncomfortable asking these types of questions? Notice how you are feeling. In time, the discomfort will go away.

By the way, no one guessed that cheese is my favorite food.

November 9, 2020 (Week 13 of School – Distance Learning)

QUESTION
How did you feel with more than two people in the breakout room?

Actual student responses (without any corrections)
– *It was fun we were talking non stop if felt better we were talking about what we do in a day,food,pets and a lot more*
– *I don't know why but I felt comfortable maybe because there was more people we talked about food and our favorite colors.*
– *It was kind of awkward because my partners were kind of quite, but then we started to make a conversation.*
– *It felt kind of awkward because the third person wasn't talking. We were talking about food and games.*
– *it was a really funny experience until someones grandma judged me*

MY INSIGHTS

I put the students in groups of three to four in the breakout rooms and did not realize that they would be more comfortable. I thought the opposite. Again, it is about asking the questions.

The student who said, "it was a really funny experience until someones grandma judged me" started a conversation about judgment.

I gave a short explanation about how we don't have control over anyone but ourselves, to calm this child down. We will talk a lot more about this next semester (after we feel much more connected). I gently said that grandparents' job is to protect their grandchildren, and maybe it is done before they know what is really going on. I asked the child how he felt and he said, "mad, embarrassed, and sad." I asked him to notice those feelings, and they will begin to dissolve.

QUESTION

What is your goal/desire for your future? What do you REALLY want to do/be?

Actual student responses (without any corrections)
– *I don't have one yet because I really don't know what I want to be.*
– *I want to succeed go to college get a job and have a great life by myself.*

– *evolve the world in to a place that humans can coexist with the
  environment and animals in order to heal the world because we
  only have one to take care of*
– *My goal is to be able to get as many scholarships and be able to
  attend the best medical school in order to be a cancer doctor.*
– *To become a nurse*
– *I want to go to college either harvard or Santa Barbara Then I
  want to become either a professional artist or become a nurse.*

MY INSIGHTS

This question was to find out a little bit more about them. I learned
about what interests them, what they think they might do in the future,
and where they might want to go to school. Questions like these are
meant to grow the connection by having the students feel comfortable
sharing stuff about themselves. Connection is a journey that needs to
be cultivated and grown.

QUESTION

How do you feel about the elections? I asked this one day after the
2020 presidential elections.
Actual student responses (without any corrections)
– *I feel a little better but I am still scared because if any of them were
  sill elected their would be things that would happen around the us*
– *I feel pretty good about the election. At fist I felt nervous for it but
  not anymore.*
– *I feel more relieved.*
– *Out of stress*
– *I don't feel anything because I don't really care about the election.*

MY INSIGHTS

This question was not really about the presidential elections, but about
how they were feeling at this moment. It was nice to see that so many

students were feeling less stressed and that they noticed it. I think that they wanted to share their feelings with anyone who wanted to listen.

November 10, 2020 (Week 13 of School – Distance Learning)

QUESTION

What did you see when I first mentioned, «See yourself when you are 25?»

Actual student responses (without any corrections)

– *I saw myself buying my parents a home and going places with my camera.*

– *me being in college and being a lawyer and having a house and being very successful.*

– *working and looking for abandoned animals and helping them be healthy.*

– *I didn't see anything since I don't expect to live that long.*

MY INSIGHTS

This question was another chance for me to connect more deeply with the students and for them to feel comfortable sharing. Almost everyone shared, and was excited to tell me their goals.

I put the students in breakout rooms to continue talking about their life so that they could also connect with other people their own age, except for the one who wrote the last response. It was a red flag for me and I told her that. She said that she meant that she only thinks about what is going on now and does not think nor plans for the future. She understood why I was concerned. After the conversation, I realized that she is angry and does not know how to deal with it. I will keep an eye on her and continue checking in with her.

If I had not been asking these questions, I would not have known how she was feeling. After the short conversation, I noticed that she is taking the meditations more seriously and is wanting to feel better.

One-on-one conversation with a failing student
QUESTION

Me: You are such a bright young man, why are you NOT doing your work?

Student: It is my laziness.

Me: I asked him to try again because I knew it wasn't laziness.

Student: I see other students struggling who are better than me and if they can't do it, I know I can't do it.

Me: I told him that there will ALWAYS be someone smarter than you and there will ALWAYS be someone less smart than you. Why are you measuring your learning against someone other than yourself? He stared at me and I knew he got it right away. I told him to see how much work he can get done today and measure it against what HE did yesterday. He looked so relieved.

MY INSIGHTS

If a teacher/parent/adult can listen with their heart and not only to the words, a deep connection and healing can happen. This student was willing to open up to me since we have been talking about our feelings for months. If we had never started the conversation, I would have never known how to talk to this student and help him through something that may be life-changing for him. How long has he felt this way? How long has this been holding back? Maybe this fear has already dissolved in him. I will continue to keep an eye on this student also. How many other students simply need someone to listen to them? Actually, how many adults simply need someone to listen to them?

QUESTION

You all look tired. Why are you so tired?

Actual student responses (without any corrections)

– *No for me its just that I have trouble going to sleep sometimes and I wake up really sleepy and tired.*

– *I can't go to sleep easily and go to sleep round 11pm-1am.*

– I am just tired from playing video games
– Yes because I get stressed and I go too sleep really late.

MY INSIGHTS

The students looked more tired than usual. Many are still struggling to sleep and I wanted to let them know that they are not alone. I suggested that they breathe deeply several times while they are trying to fall asleep to see if that helps. We also discussed that a lot of energy is used when they think a lot and when they are stressed. I reviewed with them that if they catch their fear, anxiety, or boredom, and breathe, it will help them return to calm.

QUESTION

Do you have a bedtime? What time is it?
Actual student responses (without any corrections):
– I don't have one
– Nope I don't
– no I don't have a bedtime I just go to sleep when I am tried
– Yes,I have a bedtime it is 10:00 or 10:30 but usually I stay up using my phone or watching movies.
– We go to bed at 9pm, but I don't sleep until later.

MY INSIGHTS

I am going to ask them for one day to go to bed earlier than their normal time and see what happens. The students have not connected that going to bed late will make them tired the next day. I just wanted them to be aware of the connection. They may not do anything about it, but now they have the knowledge. It will need to be repeated often, without judgment.

November 13, 2020 (Week 13 of School – Distance Learning)

QUESTION

Listen with your whole body to what your partners in the breakout

68

rooms are REALLY saying. Feel what the other person is REALLY saying. What is the hardest thing for you to do during the school day? Were you able to FEEL what they were saying?

Actual student responses (without any corrections)

– *I could listen but I couldn't feel what they were talking about.*
– *Yes, I was able to feel what the other person was saying because I do go through the same things my classmate does.*
– *Yes I could feel what the other person was saying because I could relate to them.*
– *Yes I could feel the same as the other person because we had very similar insite. It was fun.*
– *I felt a small connection while talking and we talked about hobbies and our struggle with school*
– *I was able to feel some of the ways they felt, I could really feel and relate to them about some things.*
– *I think I was because they felt stressed and overwhelmed about school and having to arrive on time everyday and I felt their stress.*

MY INSIGHTS

I had no idea how the students would feel doing this exercise. Some were able to feel something because they could relate to the situation. Most could relate, but could not feel what the other was feeling. It is a new topic that we will continue practicing.

Feeling what the other person is saying is a high-level listening skill that takes awhile to develop. I wanted to see if they could do it at such a young age. Most people do not listen. It is because they are not taught how to. Most people want the other person to hurry up and finish talking so that they can say what is on their mind. Often they are not listening at all. Also, many interrupt because they are not listening. It is not a judgment because many people just do not have the awareness.

If we can stop and fully listen, then the other person feels heard and that is something that could heal the other. [I am not talking about healing a physical issue.] Imagine how good you would feel if someone would listen to you fully. The issue that you are facing could dissolve, and you would feel healed/free of it.

I feel incredibly connected to the students this year though we are in a pandemic. I have not heard most of their voices and I do not know how tall they are but I feel closer to this group than any other class I have ever had. I love this connection and will continue asking questions even when we are back in the school building.

QUESTION
Meditation share.
Actual student responses (without any corrections)
- *During the meditation I'm pretty sure I was actually able to feel my thoughts floating.*
- *I felt mad and stressed in my head were i just want to open my eyes and cry.*
- *I feel more relaxed everytime I do this I forgot everything that is happening outside me*
- *I felt relaxed and I caught when I was irritated*
- *I could feel all the negative thoughts gone it was calming and relaxing.*
- *I calm warm in my head and felt my yellow in my heart (meaning happiness).*
- *Wow that was so craZY I want to do the meditation again it was the best one yet it felt like I didn't even move.*
- *I felt like if I was in a warm blanket.*
- *I felt really stressed the most stressed I have ever been but now I am calm.*

MY INSIGHTS
This three-minute Serene Mind meditation has opened up the floodgates of awareness. They can now verbalize what is going on,

and it is amazing. *"I am able to feel my thoughts floating . . . forgot everything that is happening outside me . . . feel all the negative thoughts gone . . . yellow in my heart. . . ."* It is almost as if they are writing poetry. It takes many adults a really long time to notice that there is stuff happening "outside" of themselves and to notice what is happening on the "inside."

November 18, 2020 (Week 14 of School – Distance Learning)

QUESTION

If you had the power to change something in the world, what would it be? Be specific. [They were in breakout rooms in small groups.]

Actual student responses (without any corrections)

– *If I had the power to change something would be covid and make it go away.*

– *If I had the power to change something in the world it would be making people treat other people equally. I would change this because I think that it is important in our world.*

– *I would change that there is no more racism anymore.*

– *To change people taking their kids away from their parents.*

– *What we shared about was noting because all of us were in fear.*

– *What I would change is society because people think of us as different.*

MY INSIGHTS

I had no idea that the shares would be so deep. So many students want to stop racism. They are so young to know what racism is, which tells me that they have already experienced it. This is another example of the students not feeling alone.

The child who said, "To change people taking their kids away from their parents" gives me an insight into her life. This will give me an opportunity to talk to her one on one to see what is going on in her life.

Most people would say that they did not share because they could not think of anything but the one student who said that they did not share because they were in fear was a HUGE insight.

Questions lead to sharing, which leads to students feeling connected and heard.

Deciding to give them something to think about, I said, "You have so many things you want to change, so why not do it in your lifetime?"

November 19, 2020 (Week 14 of School – Distance Learning)

QUESTION

Are you comfortable talking about your feelings in breakout rooms?
Actual student responses (without any corrections)

– no

– no

– no

– no

– no, not really

– nooooooo

– yes

– yes very confortable

– yes,but sometimes I don't know what i'm feeling

MY INSIGHTS

We have been discussing our feelings for about 9 weeks and I thought that they would be comfortable sharing with their peers, but my assumption was wrong. Around 80% said, "no". Again, it is all about asking the questions and finding out how the students really feel.

Imagine if I had not asked them, putting them into breakout rooms to talk about their feelings. It could have been a disaster. But since I know that I need to ask them how they feel about stuff we do, I learned something new about them. I am incredibly impressed that they knew that they were not comfortable and they were able to tell me. I am interested to see how they will respond by the end of the year. I am assuming them that they will be more comfortable.

Weeks of questioning and listening, I believe, made this student feel comfortable and safe sharing something very difficult with me. I had to hold back the tears. Here is a one-on-one conversation in the chat box that continued for a couple of weeks. I feel honored that he shared this with me.

11-19-20 From a student to me (privately):
Student: *I feel sad*
From a student to me (privately): I feel sad because my grandfather got covid and he is in the hospital
Me: I can feel your sadness.
Me: Can I share what you told me with the other teachers?
Student: *Yes*
12-2-20
Me: How is your grandfather?
Student: *He is doing better*
Student: *I think he is going to get through it because he is strong*
12-3-20
Student: *I have become more stressed*
12-10-20
Me: How is your grandfather?
Student: *He is getting better but I am worried about my dad because he went to go see him and I feel like he is going to get sick*
Me: Is he in the hospital?
Student: *Yes*
Me: If your dad wears a mask that will help tremendously. Also, think positively that your dad is healthy, and that will help.

I always ask permission to share things like this so that I can keep the trust with the student. (unless I am required by law to share because I am a mandated reporter).

I shared with my principal that students are struggling with loved ones being in the hospital due to COVID-19, and he asked me how I knew. I told him that I ask the students questions and they are now comfortable enough to share what is going on in their lives. He said that he wished more teachers could get to that point with their students. It is not a judgment; it is knowing how to connect, wanting to connect, and knowing that it is desperately needed.

November 20, 2020 (Week 14 of School – Distance Learning)

QUESTION
Share something from the Gratitude Meditation.
[Day One of this meditation.]
Actual student responses (without any corrections)
– *i felt like tears were gonna come out*
– *I noticed that when I thought of all the people who had helped me I felt really happy in my heart.*
– *It made me realize that you should appreciate the people around us and that helped us.*
– *It made me feel a little emotional because when I was younger I was a bad kid and my mom changed me to be a better person.*
– *I noticed that I had a lot of people to thank and didn't realize it till now.*
– *What came out of that meditation was tears and a lot of people to thank to.*
– *Good bye Mrs. Kotto. Thank you for being so supportive of me.*

MY INSIGHTS
So many human beings do not realize or recognize how many people have helped them in their lives. Just taking the time to notice how many are involved makes us appreciate others. Gratitude is something that is lacking in the world and if these young people can

cultivate gratitude in their lives, imagine how different the world will be when they are older.

The last comment, "Thank you for being so supportive of me" was unsolicited, but it tells me that the students are starting to notice who has been helping them. I was not looking for any gratitude. I am so impressed that it came out of a twelve-year-old.

Gratitude Meditation
From O & O Academy, modified for students.

Close your eyes, please. Breathe in deeply and exhale slowly. Stay as still as you can. Focus fully on your breath.

Today we will do a gratitude meditation. There have been so many people in the world who have helped us. Some we know, and some we don't. Let's begin.

Hold in your thoughts one person who has **nurtured you in your childhood.** It could be a parent, family member, neighbor, or even a pet. *[Pause for about 30 seconds.]*
Thank that person for being a part of your life.
Wish for their wellbeing.
Think of one person who has **inspired you to be a better human being.**
Thank that person for being a part of your life. *[Pause.]*
Wish for their wellbeing.
Think of **one person who has made you feel wanted and loved.**
Thank that person for being a part of your life. *[Pause.]*
Wish for their wellbeing.
Think of **one person who is helping you or encouraging you with school.**
Thank that person for being a part of your life. *[Pause.]*
Wish for their wellbeing.
Think of **Mother Earth; feel her in your heart.** Think of what she has done for you. For example: air to breathe, plants for oxygen, water for drinking.

Thank her for sustaining and upholding your existence. Thank her for everything she has done for you even though you have never noticed it before.

Wish for her wellbeing.

Take a deep breath in, and slowly let it out, and put a gentle smile on your face. Take another deep breath in, and gently open your eyes.

November 23, 2020 (Week 15 of School – Distance Learning)

QUESTION

Share about one person that jumped into your mind and what you thought of. [Day Two of Gratitude Meditation.]

Actual student responses (without any corrections)

– *I felt happy and one person I thought of was my mom and dad and I thought of them as making me a better person.*

– *I thought of my grandma,my mom, my best friend, and my sister, I thought of all the times they have helped my through had times.*

– *The person that came up was someone that really showed me that i have a purpose of life but unfortunately he passed away*

– *I thought of Ms.kotto for helping me through distance learning.*

– *I think of my cousin and my sister and about you because you have helped everyone.*

– *I feel like I should thank you for helping me during distance learning.*

– *What came up was sadness joy and to thank a lot of people and thank you for teaching us ms kotto.*

MY INSIGHTS

Gratitude cannot be cultivated in just one day, so we did it all week. I wanted to see how much deeper their insights would get. The first day was general thanks to people, but the second day their shares were more specific. They went from "people" on the first day to grandma, mom, best friend, sister, dad, cousin, and even me on the second day. Let us see how this unfolds on Day Three.

QUESTION

Do you ever feel like you have had enough and sometimes we need a break?

Actual student responses (without any corrections)

– *Yes Ms. Kotto you are very right sometimes I feel like to tired like if I sometimes even want to skip class cause of how tired I am.*

– *You are right, I sometimes do feel like I need a break too.*

– *You are right because it's understandable feeling highly exhausted from time to time*

– *What I think it means to me is, you have had so many things to do and still have to do so many.*

– *Just had enough means to me is to get a break..*

MY INSIGHTS

I was really tired today and I knew that if I was tired, the students were probably tired also. So, I asked the question to see if they felt the same way. Most of them did.

This is another example of connecting with students. Teachers are supposed to be a certain way, to not show their emotions to students or they can lose control of the class. But after the connection is formed, things change. I can now tell the students that I am tired and they feel compassion towards me. I have been so disconnected from students in the past and if I had told them that I was tired, they would have laughed. Now that I feel connected to the students, we have a different relationship.

The students have gone through so much this year with the pandemic, fires, distance learning, and countless other things. But I see that they are incredibly brave to share how they feel.

Today, I let the students out thirty minutes early to give them a break. They needed it and I needed it.

November 24, 2020 (Week 15 of School – Distance Learning)

QUESTION

Share about one person who jumped into your mind and what you thought of. [Day Three of Gratitude Meditation.]

Actual student responses (without any corrections)

– *I want to thank my grandpa for taking care of me and everything he has done for me if I have the chance to talk to him today.*

– *I want to thank my Grandpa for always answering my questions no matter how dumb they were.*

– *I thought of you and how you help me everyday in school and you always encourage us to do our best even through zoom. I am very thankful for having you as my teacher.*

– *Thank you for being supportive with us.*

– *I would like to thank my kindergarten teacher for helping me and believing in me.*

– *I noticed that I was visualizing everything you were saying, like mother earth, I imagined rivers, forests, and deserts*

– *My great grandma showed up in my meditation I noticed how much she impacted my life.*

– *You might not have seen it but my eyes teared up. Someone who came up on my mind was my aunt because she makes me feel special.*

– *Some of my friends showed up in this meditation, and I noticed that they have always made me feel welcomed and loved.*

– *will thank my parents for making me a better person.*

– *My Dad: Thank you for believing in me and thank you for also supporting me. Oh and Thank you Ms. Kotto and have a beautiful Thanksgiving.*

MY INSIGHTS

I have noticed that in just three days, the students have a deeper understanding of gratitude and they feel it. Many were wiping away tears and I knew that they "got it." As well as having gratitude for people, they have begun to notice Mother Earth, rivers, forests, and deserts. Some students have recognized the work that I have done for them and I hope that they will have gratitude for the rest of their teachers also.

QUESTION

Have you ever rolled your eyes at your parents? What was their reaction? What do you really mean when you roll your eyes or see someone roll their eyes?

Actual student responses (without any corrections)

– *«uhh your so boring» that prob what there saying in their mind.*
– *Yes, I have rolled my eyes at my parents mostly my mom because I get annoyed really easily and its become a habit for me to roll my eyes all the time even when I don't mean to. My mom's reaction was not very good she was not happy about it.*
– *I think it means that we are angry sad, or frustrated. for me. I roll my eyes because of the way I feel*
– *It means that the person is irritated or annoyed.*

MY INSIGHTS

I had so much fun with this question. I asked the students to do something and one young lady chose to roll her eyes at me and I saw it on Zoom. Normally, I would be angry but this time it made me laugh inside myself. I took it as a teachable moment. I told everyone to roll his or her eyes just as _____ did to me. I had them do it a few times and asked them to include an appropriate sound while they were rolling. She was annoyed and I wanted to lessen this feeling.

This was another chance I had to connect with them and explain what was really happening. I told the class that she was not annoyed at me but was taking it out on me. She has so many things going on in her life with school, distance learning, grades and the pandemic. She has not been able to catch and dissolve them yet. We all have things going on and if we are not aware of the emotions that come up, and if we do not catch them, they will come back even stronger. Most people do not have this understanding or knowledge but if you are reading this book, you now do.

Because I pointed this out, many students will start to recognize when they do roll their eyes or recognize when they are about to do it.

QUESTION

How would you feel if your child rolled their eyes at you?

Actual student responses (without any corrections)

– *I would probably be sad because they are thinking that I am very boring*
– *would probably feel offended*
– *I really don't know how i would feel mabey a bit hurt*
– *I guess I would get kind of made because of the lack of respect.*
– *I would be mad because it's disrespectful to roll your eyes at someone.*
– *it would only bring me this memory and i would laugh*
– *I wouldn't get mad because maybe there is something wrong.*
– *I would feel upset*
– *I would feel disrespected*

MY INSIGHTS

I asked this question so they could notice how they would feel if the same thing were to happen to them. Many children and adults roll their eyes or do something similar without the awareness of how the other feels. It is a habit that can be broken if they notice it.

Many children and adults are unaware of how others feel but if they can become aware, they may think twice before doing or saying something. Adults and children are unaware only because they do not know to be aware.

Many students had the same reaction about someone rolling their eyes at them. This is another example of the students feeling the same about a particular situation. They are seeing that their feelings are very similar to the rest of the class and that they are more alike than they are different. They are seeing and feeling the connection.

November 30, 2020 (Week 16 of School – Distance Learning)

I noticed that one student had been showing up late and she looked tired and sad. I had a conversation with her starting in the chat, then again after class to find out what was really going on.

11-30-20
Me: Why have you shown up late for the past two days?
Student: *I woke up late*
Student: *I couldint sleep yesterday at night I kept waking up*
Student: *maybe cause thepast few days i slept late*
Me: What is really going on?
Student: *My sisters are making me feel bad.*
Me: How?
Student: *bady shame*
Me: How does it make you feel?
Student: *mad and sad*
Me: How do you feel about your body?
Student: *bad*
12-2-20
Me: Did you thank a part of your body yesterday? Which part?
Student: *I thanked my brain for helping me learn.*
12-10-20
Me: I haven't checked in with you in a couple of days. Have you continued to thank parts of your body? I would like for you to do one organ or body part each day. Thank it and tell it why you are thanking it. :)
Student: *Yes I always thank my fingers when I do arithmetic for helping me go fast.*

MY INSIGHTS

I feel so honored that this student shared a very personal issue with me. She feels safe and connected with me because of the many conversations we have had this semester. She is noticing how she is feeling, so I wanted to give her an exercise to help her with her body image. I will teach this to the rest of the class next semester.

I asked her to start thanking one part of her body each day. For example, she can thank her heart for pumping blood. Once she can appreciate what her body does for her, it will help her dissolve her negative body image. After she practices this for a while, she will start to realize that her body helps her all the time and it will help her appreciate it.

I did this exercise a few years ago. Giving thanks to different organs over several days, I began to love my body because it works so very hard for me without asking anything in return. It was an automatic feeling of love.

December 1, 2020 (Week 16 of School – Distance Learning)

QUESTION
Give me some questions that would be fun to answer in the breakout rooms.

Actual student responses (without any corrections)
– *What do you usually do when your done with your homework?*
– *what is your hobby*
– *What's your favorite movie?*
– *How are you in school?*
– *What themed park is your favorite?*
– *what is something you do in your free time?*
– *If you could get any pet what would it be?*
– *Do you like to draw ?*
– *How has your day been so far?*
– *Do you like to listen to music?*
– *What's on your Christmas list?*

– what do you do for christmas? do you celebrate it with other family members?
– What do you like about christmas?
– What do you enjoy the most of being with your family?
– Whats your favorite game and why?
– What is your favorite hobby, and why?
– How do you see yourself in the feature,why?
– How are you doing during the pandemic?
– If you can travel anywhere where would you go and why?
– where is somewhere that you would like to visit? Why? What would you do? Would you need a translator?

MY INSIGHTS

There have been a few days where a question has not come to my mind. I tried to use a pre-thought question that did not feel right when I asked it and the students saw right through it. I did not take my own advice about letting the questions flow to me during class and I learned my lesson. The students' shares were not deep or insightful, and the conversation did not flow.

So today I decided to ask the students what questions they wanted to talk about in the chat. They came up with some kid-friendly topics. This led to great discussions in the chat.

QUESTION

How did the breakout room feel today? Did the questions help?
Actual student responses (without any corrections)
– We were talking a lot and it was mostly about where would we like to go and why.
– YES A LOT we were talking a lot and it as fun we were talking about food, dogs,fruit,soccer,gaming,art and more
– We talked alot. A persons mic didn't work but they used the chat. It didn't seem like anyone was nervous.

– This was one of the best break out rooms because we talked a lot and answered all of our questions.

– The questions did help, it was less awkward because I didn't need time to think about what I was going to ask

– Goodbye Mrs. Kotto. Thank you for making me smile, and helping me learn how to meditate properly. Thank you for making me laugh and helping me talk to people I don't really know with the breakout rooms. This is a late thank you that I wanted to say on thanksgiving.

MY INSIGHTS

Since the students chose the questions, I notice that they talked a lot more than usual, and so many of them shared a lot with me. They are becoming more comfortable and more connected with the other students. They are also slowly learning to break the fear of talking and have noticed that they are "less awkward, and not nervous." They are becoming very aware of how they are feeling.

The last comment made me tear up because he gave unsolicited gratitude and I could feel that it came from his heart. The gratitude meditation that we did last week has sunk in deep with him. He could have easily said nothing, but he chose to share.

Since the school year started, I have had students share that their loved ones have passed away and that some family members are in the hospital due to COVID-19 and other reasons. Who can these students talk to? We assume that it would be their parents. But, what if the person in the hospital is the parent and they do not know how to cope? The students' parents are trying not to cry – trying to hold it together – so that the child can be okay. But the students are struggling to cope also.

Having students share what is going on in their lives is challenging for teachers because we care deeply for each child and we hurt when they hurt. This is about the students needing to be heard especially now. Please continue to ask questions and be ready to fully listen because you may be the only person in their lives that they can talk to.

This year, I needed to put aside the math curriculum to connect with the students AND a miraculous thing has happened. I am NOT saying to stop teaching. I am saying that students need to feel connected and heard, then teach the curriculum. You will notice that amazing things happen. My students are working harder than ever. My classes were part of the Khan Academy Learn Storm challenge and we ended in second place out of ALL the schools in the United States. Learn Storm is a way to get students to practice more math and they get to see how many assignments each class completes daily. For more information: https://learnstorm.khanacademy.org/

Connection (questions, sharing, listening, feeling heard, meditating) has been the key for the students and me this year. The students are learning more and are generally more confident.

December 2, 2020 (Week 16 of School – Distance Learning)

QUESTION

Have you ever been happy for no reason?

Actual student responses (without any corrections)

– *Yes a random smile just came to me the other day.*

– *yes*

– *No not really.*

– *yes i have been it happens alot*

 – *Yes, I really like it because I also get confident*

 – *Yes and I don't know why.*

– *Nope, never the emotion that happens for no reason is sadness.*

MY INSIGHTS

We know when we are angry, sad, frustrated, and annoyed but how often do we notice when we are happy? I wanted the students to start to notice it. Since no one has taught them that they can be aware of their happiness, they did not know to do it. Now that they have this information, they can start. They do not need to know why they are happy; they can just notice it.

This is not positive thinking; it is much deeper. It is being aware of how one is feeling on the inside.

December 3, 2020 (Week 16 of School – Distance Learning)

QUESTION

Do you know an adult who is angry, mad, frustrated, or stressed a lot?

Actual student responses (without any corrections)

– *yes*

– *yes*

– *yes*

– *yes*

– *Yes I do.*

– *I actually don't*

– *yesssssssssssssssss*

– *Yes*

– *Yes*

– *no*

MY INSIGHTS

There is absolutely NO judgment in this question at all. I knew that most of the students would say that they know an adult who is almost always angry, mad, frustrated, or stressed. Most people know someone like this. This opened up a huge discussion about the importance of catching their stressful emotions.

In a nutshell, I shared that if young people don't catch their stressful emotions like fear, anger, boredom, frustration, and sadness, it will only get larger and stronger. If these twelve-year-olds can catch their feelings in the moment, they will not grow bigger and more powerful and they WILL NOT grow up to be angry adults. Imagine if all children had this information NOW.

If today's angry adults only had this knowledge earlier, then they would not be so stressed now. I wish I had had this information as a child so I would have been a much happier adult. The good thing is that I have the knowledge now (and so do you).

QUESTION
Since the beginning of this school year, have you noticed that you are more or less stressed?

Actual student responses (without any corrections)

– *I feel like i am in the middle*
– *Since the beginning I felt less stressed.*
– *I think I might be a bit more stressed.*
– *At the beginning of the year I would be extremely stressed and anxious but now I rarely feel upset and usually feel happy.*
– *I've noticed I'm less stressed.*
– *Since the beginning of school I felt more stressed but then my stress has calmed more down going more into the year*
– *I been more stressed in the beginning of the year then right now*
– *I have become more stressed*

MY INSIGHTS

This has been an incredibly stressful year with the pandemic and distance learning. This was a question to get them to reflect on all of the things we have done to help lower their stress level. I wanted them to notice that they have a choice and control over what to do when they notice what they feel. The questions helped them tremendously to recognize their emotions, share their feelings, and to be heard. The meditations helped them to be calm. The students are also sharing that they meditate on their own to be calm. I love that!

The discussion morphed into how they are helping others to be calm even if they don't mean to. If the student is at peace, then the parents can feel it (even if they do not recognize it) and they can be less stressed.

December 4, 2020 (Week 16 of School – Distance Learning)

QUESTION

What is your brain saying that makes it okay for you to not do your homework?

Actual student responses (without any corrections)

– *Before I do my homework It tells me I dont what to do it I want to watch youtube. But I push my self to do it and when I am done I just go and lay down and watch youtube.*

– *When I sometimes forget to do my homework by brain tells me to do it later and then I end up not doing it.*

– *My brain tells me that if I don't do my homework my grades will go down and I will get in trouble in class and embarrassed.*

– *I feel guilt that it's your job to do make everyone learn and me not doing it for some reason.* Me: [Interesting that they made a connection between teacher and student.]

– *I have to do ir because my brain will keep bothering me.*

– *I would say that words in my head are saying to do my homework and get stressed if I do it late and it gets me a bit overwhelmed and sometimes I try to tell myself that I need to do it early to not be so stressed.*

– *It really doesn't talk to me when I do my homework.*

– *oh I get what you are saying*

MY INSIGHTS

I told the students that I really wanted to know what was holding them back from doing their homework. I know all students want to succeed and I wanted them to notice what their brain is saying to them when they do not do their homework. I actually wanted them to catch what their brain is saying so that they could "release" the phrase.

If they can catch the thought, then it will not turn into an emotion of guilt, embarrassment, shame, or incompetence. This is an adult lesson that I learned. I thought that if I could share it with twelve-year-olds, maybe some of them would understand it now and not when they are much older. I was thrilled that one person said, "oh I get what you are saying."

QUESTION

What can you tell yourself when you hear you brain tell you, "You are going to get everything wrong anyway so why try?"

Actual student responses (without any corrections)

– *stop it I work hard.*
– *I can do it*
– *It's going to be worth it in the future.*
– *'I can do it'*
– *I can do it*
– *I've got this*
– *I am smart I got this*
– *I am smart*
– *I can do this.*

MY INSIGHTS

In my many years of teaching, I have noticed that so many students beat themselves up for making mistakes. Then their brain starts to tell them that they are not good enough or not smart enough. They begin to believe it. If students can notice and catch when their brain says these unkind things, then it can be changed. Instead of believing that they not good enough, they can start believing that they are GOOD ENOUGH!!

First, the students need to catch it, which is not easy because it has been such a habit for them for so long. Again, this is an adult lesson, but if they can learn it now, wow! This will also transform their lives in that they will not become adults who get so angry or disappointed just because of a thought that jumped into their minds.

December 7, 2020 (Week 17 of School – Distance Learning)

QUESTION
Please, tell me something that has been bothering you. If you can write it out, a lot of times it helps.
Actual student responses (without any corrections)

– *Something that has been bothering me a lot is that there's nothing to do and it feels like every single day is just repeating itself and I don't even know why but it just bothers me.*
– *Something that been bother me is that my mom only want A's and I told her that a B is also good because I currently have one and I'm trying to fix it.*
– *What bothers me is I won't do my work. My brain wants to do it saying how I am going to flunk and if I don't flunk, I will get a bad job. But I procastinate, that bothers me.*
– *I never really had really had friends because I have trust issues.*
– *Something that is bothering me is that I get some problems with my parents I get stress out I get angry.*
– *There's one thing that has been bothering me from a very long time and its being afraid to ask someone to help or do something for me because I have the fear of what they are going to say to me.*
– *Something that has been bothering me is not being able to have a normal christmas.*
– *I feel like Im dumb*
– *something that has been bothering me is that my dad is going to come home and I don't know if I should be happy or sad*

– *Well something thats bothering me is that I feel like some times people dont like me because I just talk to much or I feel like Im just annoiying people . It really just makes me overthink on how to not do that . Like I want to say so much stuff but I just dont and decide to keep it to myself.* *** [See her follow-up comment on December 16.]
– *I'm nervous about my family getting sick because of a pandemic.*
– *I've been wanting to do homework but i've been really stressed out alot and I don't know how to convince myself to do it*
– *It bothers me how fast you managed to get me to open up to you about my emotions because usually I don't open about my emotion for example my best friend I've known her for almost 4 years and I'm barely opening up to her on my feelings and emotions.*

MY INSIGHTS

I have been guiding the conversations with the questions that come to me, but today I wanted to see what was bothering them without much guidance from me. I told them that if they were able to put into words what they are feeling it would feel like a burden has been lifted from their shoulders. Wow!

I was amazed that they shared such heartfelt and deep answers. So many students do not have a place to share what they are worried about. It is just sitting inside of their hearts and growing larger. There is so much work still to do so that students come out of this pandemic not feeling alone and in depression. I will continue to ask questions and now I need to have more one-on-one conversations just to make sure every child is ok and has someone to talk to. Sometimes students need another adult in their life to just listen. The child who said, *"It bothers me how fast you managed to get me to open up to you about my emotions,"* made me laugh because the conversations and the being comfortable with sharing is working.

I work at a school where most of the students are the first in their family to go to college and I believe that many are feeling this pressure. It may not be something that they have noticed yet but it might be underlying stress. I will ask them about this next quarter to see how they feel.

I am also going to talk to many of these students one-on-one just to make sure that they are okay and so they know someone heard them.

QUESTION
How do you feel now that you shared what you shared?
Actual student responses (without any corrections)

– *Better*
– *I feel better.*
– *Relieved*
– *like you can help me with my grades*
– *I feel more relieved and more myself.*
– *Now I feel like I can convince myself that I can do it*
– *I feel less uncomfortable.*

MY INSIGHTS
While I was reading about what they were worried about, I also felt a sense of worry/urgency/need/responsibility because they are hurting inside. Therefore, I had them share how they felt after telling me what was really bothering them in hopes that it would make them feel better. It did. I asked a second question to make them feel better and it did. They noticed that they felt better after sharing.

I will continue with the questions daily because I know it is helping. This might be the only time and place that they get to share their deepest worries, fears, and discomforts.

QUESTION
[Meditation share.]
Actual student responses (without any corrections)

– *During the meditation I felt a tear running down my face and was so confused.*

– During the mediation I felt annoyed and after I feel calm.

– My breath is slower and my chest feels lighter

– During the meditation I got a feeling usually only get when I'm around those I love like my family members and I think I'm beginning to miss them.

– I had a flashback memory of when my cousin, grandma, and I went to go see IT ch. 2 and my grandma fell asleep and a scary part came up and everyone in the theater gasped and she woke up and dropped all the popcorn

MY INSIGHTS

The students shared deep and heavy emotions today. The meditation was to help them release the discomfort. I discussed with the whole class the comment "I felt a tear running down my face and was so confused." I told them that tears are GREAT because it is dissolving the "negative" emotions that come up. It is a very good thing even though it may be uncomfortable, and to not hold them back. I have noticed several students (boys and girls) wiping away tears and it makes me so happy because it is helping them, even if they do not realize it.

I included the last student's response because it was the first time this child shared anything with me. It took her seventeen weeks, but she is finally comfortable enough to open up and share.

I spend a large part of each class discussing emotions, feelings, meditating, and being in the moment and it is really paying off. I have around 90% daily Zoom attendance. Of those students, around 90% are turning in all of their homework. More important than the schoolwork, I am seeing such confidence and connections in the students. It is beautiful.

One-on-one conversation

12-7-20

Me: Please, tell me something that has been bothering you.

Student: *Something that bothers me Is that I'm missing my grandpa*

Student: *The meditation felt better because It made my emotions a little better.*

Student: *I feel sad because he past away recently.*

Me: I am so very sorry about your grandfather.

Me: How long ago did this happen?

Student: *on Friday (three days ago)*

12-10-20

Student: *Last night was a the worst cause I couldn't sleep.*

Student: *The meditation felt good help me release by stress.*

12-14-20

Student: *The meditation helped me because It made feel way better.*

12-17-20

Me: What is the number one stressful emotion that you feel?

Student: *stressed,sad,annoyed,mad,guilty,upset,lost,tired,nervous.*

Me: Why?

Student: *Because I lost someone important in my life.*

I asked the question, "Please, tell me something that has been bothering you." This student felt comfortable enough to share, he needed to share this with someone, and it was a privilege to be that person. When I read it, it took a lot for me not to cry.

I am so proud that he is NOT hiding his emotions and feelings, but sharing them with his teacher (me). Wow! He feels connected to me and this heart-breaking incident will not destroy him or stop him from learning because he has already learned to notice how he feels and because he has been meditating. The death of his grandfather is incredibly hard for this young man, but he knows how to cope and my hope is that he remembers this for the rest of his life.

December 11, 2020 (Week 17 of School – Distance Learning)

QUESTION
What did you fail at this week? Explain.
Actual student responses (without any corrections)

– l failed at catching my emotions.
– I failed at not procrastinating
– I failed to not give my parents an attitude.
– I don't remember failing at something this week? [I asked him to try again and he said. . .] I failed at being considerate of outers by wakeing up at 6 and wakeing my parants up with a rucus.
– I failed at doing a turn in my dance class because I messed up at the end of it.
– I think I failed in not really having some patients and not trusting myself. Sometimes I think that I cant do something like homework.
– This week I failed at not procrastinating I kept telling myself I'm going to do the work I'm going to get it done and in the end I ended procrastinating. Also I have horrible time management skills.
– I failed at being considerate of outers by wakeing up at 6 and wakeing my parants up with a rucus.
– Well, I failed in being in being helpful with my mom like being doing the chores. Its my duty in doing that.
– week I failed at trying to stay calm because in the beginning of the week I told myself I'm going to be calm so that i don't explode and be mean or rude but I failed, yesterday I was everything but calm.
– I failed on being happy this week
– I failed winning a game in among us with a group of friends in zoom.
– I failed at playing with my dog for more than 45 minutes I only did it for 35.
– yesterday I didn't do my khan cause I thought I had already done it and I didint even check twice so I feel like I failed.
– I failed on myself because bad memories come to my mind and start to cry.

I noticed an interesting response so I had a one-on-one conversation.

Me: How do you feel after taking the test?

Student: *I feel happy and smart*

Me: What did you fail at this week? Explain.

Student: *I failed at being a child*

Me: Please explain what you mean.

Student: *I failed on being a child because I'm not smart as my brother and sister and I'm not a good child like my sister and brother*

Student: *I felt sad for days and didn't felt to do anything i was to sad*

Me: [Meditation share.]

Student: *Can i keep it off i dont want people to see me (her video)*

I did not share what this student said to me but I told the whole class that I was so proud of ____ because she was sharing and noticing how she was feeling. It is not easy, but she is doing it. Once I said that I was proud of her, a smile broke. I think that she needed to say what was going on in her heart and have someone hear her fully because what she feels is real.

MY INSIGHTS

I asked this question to teach the students that they can – and need to – break the fear of failing. It is very difficult if no one is taught to catch the emotion when they fail.

I am noticing that more students "need" a one-on-one conversation and it is because they are opening up more and sharing deep emotions and feelings that they are starting to notice. They may have never known why are feeling a certain way, but because we are constantly discussing deep topics, and meditating, things are opening up beautifully!

Again, these students need to know that they are not alone in what they are feeling. If she is feeling like a failure, many others are feeling the same way but they are afraid to share. I know that many students could relate to what I was saying and it will also help them.

QUESTION

How did it make you feel to fail?

Actual student responses (without any corrections)

– *dissapointed*

– *Some shame and guilt.*

– *It made me feel disappointed and sad.*

– *It made me feel worthless*

– *made me feel sad*

– *It made me feel upset and dissapointed*

– *I fell like it;s going to effect me for a log time .*

– *It makes me feel like I was the only one who fail and it stressed me alot*

– *I was kind of like frustrated*

– *felt ashamed about my failure.*

– *I felt like if I was going to fail my parents*

– *I felt disappointed in myself I always feel like that when I fail.*

– *I felt dumb*

– *I felt guilty*

MY INSIGHTS

I read some of these aloud during the first class and tears fell from my eyes. Wow! I had NO idea that they were so hard on themselves. That being said, WOW! In seventeen weeks, they are able to verbalize their deep feelings. Many adults are not able to do that yet. Because of their awareness, these emotions can be dissolved over time.

I used these questions to teach the students how to break the fear of failing. It is very difficult if no one is taught to catch the emotion when they fail.

Catch it, pause, be aware, breathe, do not judge the emotion, meditate, and dissolve. This is NOT a formula; it is a way to get from feeling stressed to feeling calm. Imagine if all young people could dissolve their stressful feelings when they are young. They would become amazingly calm adults. If you are reading this for the first time, please know that this works with anyone at any age. It worked for me.

QUESTION

What happens when you can't speak up? What do you feel?

Actual student responses (without any corrections)

– I feel annoyed that I can't speak up because I'm sometimes to scared.

– I feel sick in my stomach.

– I feel nervous and I start moving my legs.

– I fee uncomfortable embarrased.

– I feel like I am going to vomit

– I what to say something and I open my mouth and nothing comes out and I just walk away knowing I could have done something.

– feel nervous and I feel pulled back and front because I want to say something but I cant at the sametime

MY INSIGHTS

I struggled with speaking up because of a deep fear inside of me. I do not wish that on anyone. I have noticed that several students struggle also. I would love to help them break that pattern in their life. If they can notice it and not judge it, then over time, it will dissolve. It has dissolved tremendously for me, so I know it is possible.

QUESTION

[Meditation share.]

Actual student responses (without any corrections)

– The meditation was very relaxing and my mind took me to a place near the ocean.

– During the mediation I only had happy thoughts about things that made me happy like my friends.

– After the meditation I felt like I wanted to do all my work and I felt energetic.

– My eyes were kinda watery.

– At first I felt annoyed then I felt relaxed

– I felt very comfortable and relaxed I felt like something was in my stomach and it felt beautiful.
– My head took me to the future, when I go to college.
– I felt giggly because my mind took me to when I failed breakfest because we were talking about failing and I felt like laughing
– I started releasing stuff about my past.

MY INSIGHTS

Each time we meditate, I notice how much calmer the students get and how much easier it is for me to teach them. Oh, that is a HUGE benefit to meditation. Once the students' minds are calm, learning is so much easier because their mind is not cluttered with thoughts. I highly recommend it if your school allows it. If they do not, then have them breathe deeply a few times with their eyes open which is one way to help them to be a little calmer.

"I started releasing stuff about my past." I am impressed that she is noticing this and is able to put it into words. She has not shared much about what happened in her past, but she has shared often that there is stuff in her past that bothers her.

December 14, 2020 (Week 18 of School – Distance Learning)

QUESTION
Are you ever afraid to ask teachers questions?
Actual student responses (without any corrections)
– No because I don't even think about being scared when I ask a question.
– yes because depending on the question I feel like they will get mad at me
– Yes because I feel like they might get mad.
– No not really because teachers are meant to be there to help us with any questions.

– *Yes, because I sometimes think they will get mad at me for not paying attention.*
– *Yes. I feel like i'm afraid to ask them questions because I feel like I should already know and that I don't need to ask for help.*
– *yes because I don;t want to annoy*
– *Yes because I think whatever the question is it will be disrupting the class or something my teacher doesn't want to fix*
– *Yes I have sometimes felt afraid to ask because they either explained what I needed to know and I didnt wanna ask but also because I think their gonna think something about me*
– *Yes because Im afraid of what they are going to say*
– *Yes because I feel like when I try to ask them I don't know how to say it.*
– *I get afraid to ask teachers questions because I feel like they will be like. We just went over that your should've payed attention.*

MY INSIGHTS

Something interesting happened to me a few days ago and that is why I asked this question to see if it was only my issue, or a student issue also. I needed to ask my IT person a question about a standardized test that I was going to give the students. A funny sensation came over me right as I was going to send him an email. I got scared and nervous. I honestly thought that he was going to get mad at me. It was irrational but interesting at the same time. I notice my feelings, became calm, then sent the email. He answered my question and did not get mad.

It was the weirdest thing, so I asked, "Are you ever afraid to ask teachers questions?" I was amazed and shocked that so many of them said that they thought we would get mad. I had no idea that kids felt this way. After reading their answers, it led to the next question.

QUESTION

How do you feel right before you ask a teacher a question?

Actual student responses (without any corrections)

– *Nervous*

– *I feel nervous*

– *I feel paranoid and scared*

– *I feel Scared/nervous/afraid*

– *I feel nervous*

– *I feel very scared*

– *I feel nervous, even around teachers I trust, I always feel nervous.*

– *I feel confused because I obviously haven't had my question answered.*

– *narvous*

– *I feel nervous and anxious.*

– *I feel scared I feel that the teacher might judge me though I know they won't.*

– *I feel nervous sometimes I get really shy.*

– *my hary starts betting really fast and I think about what the other people are saying about me and if they are calling me mean names or is they think I am dumb.*

MY INSIGHTS

I had to hold back tears while writing this. I asked the question and I had no idea that they felt this way. Again, it is all about asking questions even if we think we know the answers. If you can notice that you are afraid of asking questions, it can go away! I reminded them to notice their feelings, pause, breathe, and the emotion will begin to dissolve.

We also discussed that fear is holding them all back from succeeding. If they really do not know something and they are afraid to ask, how will they learn? They need to break free from the fear of asking questions. This discussion led to the next questions. Again, these questions were not scripted; they just came to my mind.

QUESTION

What do you think I mean when I say, "DEMAND TO BE TAUGHT?"

Actual student responses (without any corrections)

– *like we are asking to be taught..*

– *You mean that we have to be assertive and we have to do whatever we can to go to school.*

– *I think you mean that nothing is holding us back and that we can succeed.*

– *I think you mean even if we are shy we could <u>melt</u> it and go ask or go do the thing bravely*

– *To ask the questions you feel the need to be answered, I think.*

– *I think you mean That you have to feel free to ask anything.*

MY INSIGHTS

"Demand to be taught" means to ask questions when you do not know something, even if you are afraid, so that you can learn. This is about dissolving emotions that do not serve us so that nothing stands in our way of being calm and happy. If fear is standing in your way of learning what you need to learn, then it needs to melt away (as one student said in the student responses).

December 15, 2020 (Week 18 of School – Distance Learning)

QUESTION

Do you ever feel like school is not worth it? Explain, please.

Actual student responses (without any corrections)

– *yes,because school is the most part of me getting stressed but I also have to accomplish my goals*

– *no because you can have a talent you never knew in one of the classes.*

– *Yes, all the time, while I work I just get a sudden wave of emotion of reality and sadness because who knows if I'm going to college.*

– Yes, I feel like school sometimes is not worth it because I sometimes tell myself that I wont make it, I wont get me dream job, I wont be rich, so what is the point.

– Yes, because how is learning how to do multiplication and learning about the mitochondria going to help me in the real world. But that still doesn't mean I'm not going to try in school.

– I honestly just wish schools taught adult life like taxes, housing, and jobs.

– Yes because I get stressed and very sad.

– Yes because some subjects are useless like they teach us that the leaves are green because of chlorophyll but they don't teach us how to pay taxes

– Sometimes yes, I do feel like school is not worth it. It makes me feel so many negative emotions that I sometimes end up taking out all those emotions on my little brother.

– yes I meet know friends and I get to make memories with them.

MY INSIGHTS

This question came to my mind during class and many said that they feel like school is not worth it because of the stress. They do not see the connection between what is being taught and what they think they will need in the future.

Some students commented on life skills such as taxes. I asked them if they had a job and were paying taxes. They laughed because they are only twelve and they do not currently have a job. I hear students say, "Why do we have to learn this?" Sometimes it's hard to explain why they need to learn certain stuff. I had fun with one person's comment: *"Yes because some subjects are useless like they teach us that the leaves are green because of chlorophyll but they don't teach us how to pay taxes."* The discussion turned into a bunch of questions to get them to be interested and to think. If you know that plants are green because of chlorophyll, why not take it a step further and be curious and ask yourself questions like "Could I make chlorophyll yellow, and if so would the leaves be yellow? How cool would it be if leaves were pink? If I could change the color of leaves, could I also change the color of the ocean, sky, or clouds?" I could see their wheels turning and we had fun.

If students can be curious, then learning is not seen as a chore or boring. Since I teach math, I asked the next question to see what they would come up with.

QUESTION
Why are fractions important?
Why do I have to learn about fractions?
Actual student responses (without any corrections)
- *To divide your money if you ever own a business and you have employees.*
- *In the future it will be needed for all the things like taxes and many more things*
- *Fractions are used in many things including business, baking, and even science.*
- *because when we have kids and they need help we can help them*
- *to subtract certain amounts of my future paycheck to pay bills*

MY INSIGHTS
Students struggle with fractions. This question opened up a great math conversation. I told them that they will use fractions in their life and I gave them two reasons that jumped into my mind. The first was that they would need to know how to use fractions for higher-level math, which in turn will help them get better grades and help them get into college. They did not seem to care much about that answer so I gave them one that they could relate to more easily. Much later in life, when they become parents, they will need to know how to do fractions so that they can easily help their own kids. Wouldn't it be

great if someone could help you with fractions now? They liked that answer better. This led to the next question.

QUESTION

How can you be curious at school?

Actual student responses (without any corrections)

– *I dont really know*
– *I think that for most kids today it's not about learning but instead trying to actually pass their classes*
– *Maybe saying something while you're teaching math like , 'blah blah can get you into blah blah', like math to hair or engineering.*
– *I can pay more attention to details of things we learn so that we can dig deeper and be curious.*
– *Ask a question to myself if what would happen if this gets in this or think of how it would change*
– *I can be curious at school by asking random questions that seem interesting about the subject that we are learning or the subject that we are talking about.*
– *I can be curious bye thinking about things more. bye seeing what else I can find out about the subject.*
– *I can be curious at school by asking my self questions*
– *Thank you Ms.Kotto for getting me curious about curiosity.*

MY INSIGHTS

I had no idea what they would share about cultivating curiosity. If students are not curious about the subject matter, school becomes incredibly boring and feels like a waste of their time. After discussing chlorophyll and fractions it was interesting that so many talked about asking questions to become more curious.

I will try to make more connections like what this student shared, *"Maybe saying something while you're teaching math like , 'blah blah can get you into blah blah', like math to hair or engineering."* If I cannot figure out why students need to learn a specific skill, I will ask them what they think.

Remember, all of these questions are to build a stronger connection and bond with the students. It almost does not matter what you ask as long as you are asking something and are being genuinely interested in what they are sharing. Sometimes the questions elicit emotional insights or responses, but other times it is just to get them to share so that they feel like they are part of the conversation.

December 16, 2020 (Week 18 of School – Distance Learning)

QUESTION
When your brain says, «I don't want to do it,» what do you say or do?

Actual student responses (without any corrections)

– *I just do it.*
– *I have to do it it's not an option.*
– *I will probably do bad on whatever I am doing*
– *I try to fight it by moving but then I become lazy and forget about it.*
– *When my brain says «I don't wanna do it» I tell myself «but I have to»*
– *I can do it*

MY INSIGHTS
Students often struggle to start their work and often it is because they get a thought like, "You don't have to do it now; you can do it later," and they listen to it without even recognizing it. If they can just catch the thought, it loses its power. It is all about noticing the thought. Awareness is the key!

QUESTION
Tell me something that you succeeded in during the first semester of distance learning.

Actual student responses (without any corrections)

– *Something that I've succeeded in the first semester of distance learning was know how to add positive and negative numbers.*

– *I thought I couldn't do subtracting negative fractions.*

– *I didn't really do anything i am prod of last semester but this semester is when I did everything right*

– *I raised my grades so I don't have any F's anymore*

– *Not giving up and still going to school.*

– *Im proud of from when I had a F and now that iv'e been doing all my work my grade has been going up ever since and now I have a B+.*

– *im am proud that i get to learn because most people get this opportunity that we get*

– *This semester I have been proud how far I've come in math.*

– *Nothing because I feel like I could improve a lot more in my grades*

MY INSIGHTS

So often the focus is on what students haven't done or can't do and I wanted them to notice what they did "right". There are a lot of things to be proud of, but we don't focus on them. They have come a LONG way in just eighteen weeks. Each student needs to recognize that. If they can begin to notice the positive more than the negative, it will help them tremendously. Wouldn't it be great if students – if people – focused more on the positive than on the negative?

Their comments focused mostly on school, which is only one aspect of who they are. I told them that they are much more than just what they are doing in school so I asked them a follow-up question.

QUESTION

What have you succeeded in (are proud of), not related to school?

Actual student responses (without any corrections)

– *Something I am proud of that is not school is learning how to paint.*

- I am proud that I have been able to make lots of different kinds of baked goods successfully.(Cakes, Pie, cookies, muffins)

– I am proud of how much I have advanced in dance.

– I am proud that my family is safe and well

– So me and my dad go biking every saturday up a hill the first time I didn't make it all they way up. Then the next I went higher and then the third I made it ll the way up.

– I am proud that I know how to bake now

– I am proud of being a bit more independent

*– I am proud of keeping my head up no matter what happens and loving myself the way I am. Also knowing my worth and learning from my mistakes. That is what I am proud of this year.*** [See the previous comment from the same student on December 7.]

MY INSIGHTS

The students easily shared what they succeeded in at school, but they struggled a bit with this question. I had to remind them that they are much more than their grades and school work. I am not sure if everyone fully understood that school is only one part of who they are. I started to share (without their names) examples of what students wrote and more students were able to "see" themselves outside of school.

I made a BIG deal about the child who said, "I am proud of keeping my head up no matter what happens and loving myself the way I am. Also knowing my worth and learning from my mistakes. That is what I am proud of this year." She has been struggling with being okay with who she is. I almost started dancing! My arms were actually flailing when I said, "YES!! YES!! YES!! YES!!" to this student without revealing who she was. I saw a huge smile on her face and relief that she can truly feel ok with who she is.

It is all about conversations, listening, and connecting with young people. It may be one child at a time who gets to accept herself just the way she is. Imagine what a life-changing realization it is for her.

She will not have to live her life thinking that she is not good enough or that she has to change anything to feel accepted by others. WOW!!! If all adults had this insight as a child, imagine how much happier we would feel.

I spent a large part of today talking with the students. I even shared what I was proud of because a student asked me. I shared with them my terror about using Zoom.

When we went to distance learning, I called my principal and tears were jumping out of my eyes because I just did not understand the technology nor Zoom, and I did not think I could learn it. I felt like I was a brand new teacher again. He calmed me down and now I am the queen of Zoom. I am so proud of myself for learning it and being somewhat of an expert at it. I am also teaching others how to maneuver in Zoom.

It is not easy for teachers to admit faults to students. But if students can see teachers as human beings with the same feeling and emotions, they can begin to relate and connect more easily.

December 17, 2020 (Week 18 of School – Distance Learning)

QUESTION

List the stressful emotions that you have felt. List when you have felt icky, stressed or yuck.

Actual student responses (without some spelling corrections)

a bad human being, a burden, a menace, afraid, alone, anger, angry, annoyed, anxiety, anxious, ashamed, bashful, blue, bossed around, breakdown, breaking down, broken, Broken down, challenged, cold, confused, denial, depression, depressed, disappointed, discouraged, disgust, disgusted, distress, distress, down, drained, dumb, embarrassed, emotionless, emotional, empty, enclosed, enraged, failed, failure, falling apart, fearful, feel like a loser, feel without a heart, feeling down, feeling like trash, frightened, frustrated, frustration, furious, garbage, giving up, gloomy, grief, grumpiness, guilt, guilty, gullible, hangry, hated, hateful, helpless, hopeless, hurt, icky, idiot, ignored, immature, in the way of everyone, Insecure, irresponsible, irritability, irritated, like I need to protect myself from everyone, livid, lonely, lost, lost in my own mind, mad, menace, miserable, misunderstood, nervous, not confident, not confident in myself, not good enough, not worth it, numb, outcaste, overthinking, overwhelmed, pain, pointless, pointless is like you aren't important, procrastinating, punching bag, rejected, restlessness, rushed, sad, sadness, scared, self-conscious, shattered, shy, sick, smad, sorrow, stressed, stupid, tired, traumatized, troublemaker, troubled, turned down, uncomfortable, unfocused, ungrateful, unhappy, unneeded, unsecured, untrusted, unuseful, unwanted, upset, useless, weak, without purpose, worthless, your fault

MY INSIGHTS

I feel like the students are saying, *"Hear Us Now!!"* without using these exact words. Can you believe what they are sharing? Does it hurt your heart?

It hurts my heart to see so many emotions that twelve-year-old children feel. They need an outlet to heal their hearts and that is why having them share and feel like they have the same feelings as others is important. I am sure that when I was reading these words out loud and making a list, it made some of the students feel included and validated. Many times, young people feel like they are the only ones having a stressful feeling. Now, my students know that we have the same "icky" feelings inside from time to time. They are not alone.

It broke my heart to read words like "ignored," "feeling like trash," "a burden," "garbage," "hated," "hopeless," "ignored," "in the way of everyone," "outcast," "unwanted," and "worthless". They are only twelve years old.

This was a difficult discussion with the classes because it brought up many uncomfortable emotions, but it was amazing because the students were able to verbalize what they felt or had felt before. In order to heal, the emotion needs to be recognized, named (if possible), and felt.

Most adults have not recognized these deep emotions yet. If you are reading this book, maybe you can start to notice how you feel also. It is not easy. But it heals.

QUESTION
Why do you think you have felt these stressful emotions?
Actual student responses (without any corrections)
– *because I feel that no one will never help me in my life*
– *It's kind of a hard topic for me to talk about but I guess it's because I don't like my appearance that much.*
– *I think I feel that way because online school was different for me and I think it sucked me all up and left me anxious, scared and lost.*
– *I'm self conscious of how I look.*
– *Overwhelmed is my number one stressful emotion because I feel like giving up and that the stress will never end.*
– *I feel self conscious because these days your either supposed to be*

skinny or chubby
– *And angry because my brother thinks these emotions are jokes or wanting attention.*
– *Unmotivated, everyday is the same and I feel drained, everything that I used to love doing now feels like a chore.*
– *because... p u b e r t y*
– <ins>*I feel these things because I never have some to talk about them.*</ins>
– *because all my problems are like water so thats why i feel like i am drowning in my on mind*
– *Because I lost someone important in my life.*

MY INSIGHTS

Again, these shares were so hard for me to read. I think they were hard for the students to share, too, but once they did, they felt like a weight had been lifted off of their shoulders. Students carry so much stuff with them. If they could just share it with someone, it makes a world of difference in their lives. They may not feel like they can share with parents, so teachers are a good "substitute." Besides, parents may not know what to say. It is not a criticism. Students need to be able to share and have someone listen to them especially now! I continue to ask questions and am amazed at the deep, heart-felt issues they want and are willing to share with me.

So many students shared their, "why" and were eager to do so. These feelings are very real and intense. It's hard not to become emotional reading, *"<ins>because I feel that no one will never help me in my life.</ins>"*

We discussed this comment: *"And angry because my brother thinks these emotions are jokes or wanting attention."* I told the class that many people might pick on them because they have been taught to not discuss emotions. Often, it is because they are afraid to notice what is going on inside of them. After all, it is so uncomfortable. Instead of noticing their own feelings, they are lashing out at others. I told them that being aware of their own emotions is all about their own self and if they want to have a calm and happy life, this is one way to do it. If

112

others pick on them, they need to notice how it makes them feel on the inside so that it can dissolve.

I have also noticed a pattern in their comments that I would not have noticed if they had not been so willing and open to share. Several body image issues came up, which we will talk about next quarter.

Again, I ask, I listen, we share, they feel heard and therefore, they are more willing to open up and share things that have never been shared with anyone. This journey includes patience and consistency.

QUESTION
List some beautiful feeling that you have experienced.

Actual student responses (without some spelling corrections)

adventurous, amazed, angel, awesome, beautiful, blessed, brave, brave, bubbly, calm, caring, cheerful, chill, comfortable, confidence, confident, content and cheerful, cool, ecstatic, empathy, encouraged, energetic, energized, enthusiastic, excited, exuberant, fabulous, faithful, fearless, feel like I can do anything, fortunate, friendship, full of life, funny, generous, genius, gleeful, good, grateful, gratitude, happiness, happy, heavenly, helpful, hope, hopeful, in peace, independent, invincible, jolly, joy, joyful, kind, kindness, knowing, knowledgeable, laughter, like earning money for the first time by working, lovable, love, loved, lucky, merry, motivated, needed, non-stressed, not alone, not embarrassed, not lonely, noticed, over joyed, owning a house, peaceful, positive, powerful, pride, proud, recognized, relaxed, relieved, respected, respectful, rested, safe, satisfied, self-acceptance, selfless, showing pleasure, smart, strong, sweet, talented, the feeling that you did something right and that you are happy, thoughtful, thrilled, trust, trusted, unstoppable, useful, wanted, warm, welcomed, wonderful, you just did something new, your having fun I done know what it's called

MY INSIGHTS

It was harder for the students to notice the beautiful feelings that they have experienced in their lives. They listed 130 stressful emotions very quickly. It took some time for them to discover the 106 beautiful feelings. Maybe they have noticed the "icky" feeling more often and have not been taught to notice the "good" feelings.

I gave them homework over the winter break. They had to notice one stressful and one beautiful feeling every day. I told them NOT to write it down, just to notice it. I am hoping that a lot will do this exercise because if they can notice both of them throughout the day, the beautiful states will happen more often and the stressful ones will happen less often.

Right now, most people/students spend 80%-90% of their day stressed and only 10%-20% of their day in beautiful states. Once they start to notice how they are feeling, the percent begins to slowly change to 70% stress and 30% beautiful and, in time, 50% stress and 50% beautiful. Since the students are so young, this change could happen fairly quickly.

When I first started, I was living my life with at least 90% stress and 10% in calm. By noticing the emotion and meditating, I am currently around 10% stressed and 90% calm. If it can work for me, it can work for anyone. I do not want my students to become adults who are stressed 90% of the time. That is why I am sharing this information and writing this book.

"We have not paid attention to our inner state. We never thought it was important to live in a beautiful state. This has not been a part of our formal education, but it needs to be."
- Krishnaji, Co-founder of O & O Academy

Author's note:

This is the end of the first semester. Everything that I have shared in this book has been stuff that has worked for me and countless others. It now needs to be shared with young people.

With all of the questioning and connecting that has gone on this year, I wish for all students to come out of this pandemic feeling okay and connected to themselves and to others. I wish for them to not feel alone or depressed. I wish for them to feel confident and secure with who they are and who they want to be in the future. I also wish for them to share this knowledge with others. I wish that everyone reading this book can do and feel the same.

The ultimate goal is to "HEAR US NOW!" Students need to be heard in order to feel important, secure, confident, and okay. This book is not just to be used during the pandemic. Please use any of the ideas in this book when we get back into the classroom. You will see that teaching and learning improve tremendously.

The information in this book will also help parents connect more deeply with their children. My unsolicited advice to all parents is to ask questions and listen to their children NOW or as soon as possible. Many children want to be heard. Parents are incredibly important in the process. If parents can notice how they feel while their child is talking, they can also dissolve the emotions that come up in themselves. This is called the art of listening. It is a skill that can be learned and mastered with practice. I will share more during Quarter Three (this book is being written in real time so I cannot write or share about the art of listening until I see how it works with the students). For now, be in the moment when your child is talking, listen, and notice how you are feeling. Do not judge it, just notice.

Share this information with anyone willing to put down their phone, get off the internet, and step out of their comfort zone to really listen to young people.

QUARTER THREE

Let us continue and deepen our journey of connection with students and see where it takes us. Please remember that this is ONE way to connect with students and many teachers are doing such a beautiful job already. Some teachers need this information just until it becomes second nature to them. Another important reminder is that this is a SLOW process, but incredibly important. If you are reading this book now and it is the middle of the year, please start where you are.

January 13, 2021 (Week 19 of School – Distance Learning)

Quarter 3 began with what I thought were two simple questions. "Share something good that happened to you during the break, please." And "Share something not so good from the break that happened to you." I was NOT ready for their "not so good" answers.

Actual student responses (without any corrections)

– *Yesterday my grandpa died*
– *I got burned*
– *i didnt go to mexico and didnt see my gramma and she passed away.*
– *Something not so good was that a lot of hot oil fell on me and it burned me.*
– *My uncle died from covid-19*

– My friend and his family got covid.
– All my family caught covid, and my aunt died from it.
– went to my grandpa grave
– My dad and brother went to mexico cause my aunt/dads sister died and my grandpa is sick not from covid but heart problems
– Something not so good that happened was that me and family got covid and my mom had to go to the hospital and she is still there.
– My grandma was sick and she died a couple days ago and yesterday we had a funeral for her.
– Something that was not so good that happened to me over the break was that my grandma is sick, but were hoping its not corona.
– my aunts puppy died yesterday
– Nothing good happens during the break

MY INSIGHTS

The students were very willing to share their difficult life situations with me because we have already built a strong connection during the first two quarters. They felt safe and comfortable sharing. My heart broke for every one of these students. We did not talk about their shares since it was so intense for me. During the week, I spoke to each of the students one-on-one to see how they were doing. At times, we cried together and at times, I just listened. Even though it was very difficult to hear what was going on with the students, imagine how the students feel if they do not have someone to talk to?

So often, a child tries to be strong for the parent and the parent tries to be strong for the child. In this situation with me, they could cry and let it out. For us to cry together shows a deep connection and it only worked because we have been building this for months.

Today's meditation was to breathe deeply five times all the way to their tummy with their eyes open, without others noticing that they were breathing. Often, students are stressed and cannot stop to meditate so I wanted to give them a tool to help them return to a beautiful state.

Remember, there are only two inner states (feelings) that we can live in: a beautiful, peaceful state or a stressful, uncomfortable state.

I do not want to sound arrogant; however, it surprised me that no other teacher knew about these situations. One teacher said that she wants the students to connect more with her, and I love that. I told her to start small and slowly to build the rapport. It is a journey, not a sprint. I have also realized that many teachers need to be more connected. After I got permission from a student to share, I sent an email to a teacher, and all I got as a response was, "thank you".

This signals to me that many teachers are very disconnected from their own feelings and do not realize that they need to emotionally connect with their students. Again, it is not a judgement; it is an observation. Many adults, teachers included, are in survival mode when they are teaching and to add one more thing to their plate is often too much.

One of my realizations during today's discussion is that students need to talk and share with more people than just me. Therefore, I am putting them in groups of three or four so that they will have a peer to lean on for the rest of the year. They will talk, listen, help with math, help with school, and just be there for each other. While I was having them choose people for their group, one student wrote, *"i dont have no one :("* Again, this broke my heart. I will make sure this child does not feel so alone. Luckily, another student chose her to be in her group.

This whole year is about connecting to students by making them feel safe, calm, and included. To make sure that all students feel this way, I will begin one-on-one conversations with everyone. Usually, I catch up on emails while they are in their groups, but for now that can wait. I will talk to one or two children daily while others are in their breakout rooms. It will take about three to four weeks to connect with everyone, then I will start again. This is just one more way to deepen our connection. I will let you know how it goes.

One-on-One Conversations:

I connected with about six students and learned that many of their grandparents passed away. I asked them how they were feeling. All of them were sad. I reminded them to notice their sadness and to cry and cry and cry, even if other family members hold back their tears. I also reminded them that they have the knowledge about how to dissolve their stressful emotions by catching their feelings, not judging them, and breathing. I also shared that they will feel better in time. More than anything, they just wanted to talk and to be heard.

I spoke with one student who was on the verge of tears. She shared that her whole family was sick and that her mom was still in the hospital with COVID-19. Imagine how she feels being only twelve and having the most important person in her life in the hospital. We cried together. I told her that she could help by "pretending" to breathe for her mom. I wanted to give her something to do instead of focusing on the negative, and breathing deeply calms people down. I could see her breathing and she felt so much better. Luckily, her mom came home a couple of days later. She thanked me for listening and helping. Connection!

I talked to a few more students who were in class and who shared that they were positive for COVID-19. I am so impressed that they showed up to class and I told them how proud I was of them. They shared that they were scared when they found out they were positive, but they are all doing fine now.

As I was reading the student's shares again, a question came to my mind. If this were a predominately white, upper-class school, would so many of the students be dealing with so much death? The majority of the students are socioeconomically disadvantaged, Spanish-speaking, living in multi-generational households, and having parents who need to work to survive. Most probably do not have great health care. I do not feel qualified to go deep into this topic of **inequity**, but it is a shame that I am able to point it out from the twelve-year-old children's comments.

My goal is to have the students come out of this pandemic free of the side effects of depression and feeling connected and calm. If I can share this **inequity** then maybe a conversation can happen and maybe things can begin to change because they need to change NOW!

Meditation: Breathing deeply with eyes open

January 15, 2021 (Week 19 of School – Distance Learning)

QUESTION

Do you feel a lot of pressure? From where?

Actual student responses (without any corrections)

– *I feel pressure from my parents a lot.*
– *Not at the moment.*
– *Yes from school because I need to do all my work and I feel pressured to get good grades.*
– *I feel pressure because this time I want to get good grades.*
– *Currently I don't feel any pressure in my body yet.*
– *I feel like there is some pressure but most i'm just so overwhelmed from all over my body.*
– *I've been feeling a bit pressured from my parents because it seems that whenever I accidentally make a mistake or don't do something good enough they get mad or upset with me.*
– *I don't really feel pressured and if I do I usually just go on with it.*
– *I feel a lot of pressure in school.*
– *yes I do feel pressure to keep my gardes at a A or I will be mad at myself.*

MY INSIGHTS

This question came to me about pressure and I wanted to see their reactions. I was surprised to see that only a few answered and I think it is because they did not understand the meaning of "pressure." Some thought it was a physical feeling in the body. Others noticed that it was an inner state (feeling/emotion inside of their body). I was referring to their emotions. The students have not recognized that feeling yet, so we will talk more about it next week. I am sure that they have felt pressure in some form but have not been able to name it. They will have to notice the emotion first before it can begin to dissolved.

Meditation: One-minute listening.

January 19, 2021 (Week 20 of School – Distance Learning)

QUESTION
Tell me one not so good thing that happened to you this weekend.
Actual student responses (without any corrections)

– *An earthquake happened while I was taking my food down the stairs.*
– *I spilled my drink when the mini earthquake happen*
– *I had never felt an earthquake in my life it was weird watching the walls move on their own*
– *I felt very overwhelmed and scared not gonna lie, it was more close to me because I was very close by.*
– *I was in the living room when my dad told me not to freak out because there was an earthquake happening it felt cool I was surprisingly not scared.*
– *It felt weird and it also sounded like someone was breaking in also pictures were moving and doors were moving and it felt scary.*
– *I was on facetime with my cousin and she yelled «there's an earthquake» and we both started to freak out !!!*

MY INSIGHTS
We had a 4.5 earthquake over the weekend. I have to admit again that I started laughing when the student shared, *"An earthquake happened while I was taking my food down the stairs."* I could not help myself. She gave me permission to share and I apologized for laughing. I told her that I was picturing her walking down the stairs with a bowl of soup and that everything was shaking. I do not know why it was so

funny but it got the whole class laughing as well as this student. We all bonded over an earthquake, stairs, and soup.

I asked the students if they caught their feeling of being scared and many of them said, "yes". I am so impressed that they are practicing what I am teaching them. I am equally impressed that one student shared, ". . . *I was surprisingly not scared"*. I told the class that I was scared and that I did NOT catch the fear in the moment. This is still a work in progress. Some days I catch a lot and some days I do not notice any.

I also shared that right now they may have a hundred stressful feelings each day that they do not notice. Once they start to notice only one, the rest become so much easier to catch. They will go from feeling stressed 80% of the time and calm only 20% of the time to 70% stressed and 30% calm, then in time 20% stressed and 80% calm. When I first starting to catch my stressful feelings, I was probably, 90% stressed during the day but now I am around 90% calm and in a beautiful state.

This week I started to include an extra homework assignment where they are to notice one icky feeling and one beautiful feeling each day. They do not need to write it down, just notice it. In a couple of weeks, I will ask them to start writing them down so they can see how much they will progress over time.

Meditation: Serene Mind

January 25, 2021 (Week 21 of School – Distance Learning)

QUESTION

Were you able to share your icky feelings? Why or why not?
Actual student responses (without any corrections)
- *yes because I can forget that feeling when I share it.*
- *No because I usually keep my emotions to myself and I don't like to share.*
- *I wasn't able to share my icky feeling because if I did it would be my first time tell someone else other than you and since it was my first I was nervous*

– Yes, because there my friends and I trust them
– I did because I believed in myself.
– yes I was able to share my feelings because I trust them and
  they understand
– Yes because I wanted to express my feelings to other people and
  it was pretty easy.
– no because i don't feel ancontrabel sharing my feelings
  (comfortable)

MY INSIGHTS

To refresh everyone's memory, when I use the work "icky" I am referring to the uncomfortable feelings we all have at times. They include fear, anger, frustration, jealousy, and any emotion that is uncomfortable for you. When I refer to beautiful feelings, they include emotions like calm, peaceful, and happy. These are inner feelings that are comfortable.

I put the students in breakout rooms of about three people and asked them to share how they were feeling. My goal was to for them to have someone else to talk with other than me.

Here is another example of me assuming that the students would be comfortable sharing their feelings with their peers since we have been doing it for many weeks. Some were comfortable sharing and a lot were not. This opened up a huge discussion.

I told the students that they would never need to share their feelings with anyone if they were not comfortable. All you need to do is catch the icky feeling as soon as it comes up, sit in the discomfort, breathe, and in time, it dissolves. They were relieved that they did not have to share.

QUESTION

Are you catching your icky and beautiful feelings? How often?
Actual student responses (without any corrections)
– I catch two about a day being grumpy or sad.

– I catch being really unmotivated
– I catch being sad and mad
– I always forget when I am mad but I get really mad at my video games.
– yes I am am catching feeling bored stressed pressured
– Yes I catch them then I breathe and it makes me feel better
– No and not that often.
– I catch it every 1 to 2 days a week
– Not really
– Yeah, Im catching am icky feeling and a beautiful feel very often.
– I do it sometimes when I feel like yelling.
– I do not pay attention to my feelings
– I do it but it is very rare for me to do it.

MY INSIGHTS

I want the students to start catching their "icky" feelings, not just in math class, but also throughout the day so they can start to diminish. Many of the students told me that they simply forget so as a reminder, I included it in their homework. I shared with them that many adults struggle to notice their feelings and that it is not easy at first. But in time, it gets easier. I have a very good friend who is a doctor and she forgets to catch her stressful feelings during the day, too. That being said, since they all have this knowledge, they need to start noticing it. Once they catch the first one, it gets much easier and quicker.

Again, my goal is to have ALL students come out of this pandemic as calm as possible. This will also work when students are back in the building if teachers and students have this knowledge and will share this knowledge.

Here is an actual homework assignment to help them remember.
Marker: Name, Date, AND Number your problems, upload facing up, SHOW ALL WORK
M: AND . . . catch one icky feeling and one beautiful feeling... don't write it down... simply notice them...:)

page 1 # 27-29
page 2 # 21-24
page 9 # 21-24
page 10 # 1-4
page 11 # 1-4
AND... catch 1 icky feeling and 1 beautiful feeling... don't write it down...
simply notice them...:)

Meditation: Today I had them do the one minute listening meditation and it really calmed them down.

January 26, 2021 (Week 21 of School – Distance Learning)

QUESTION
Share something with me that you are worried about.
Actual student responses (without any corrections)
– *I'm worried about my health and my family's health.*
 – *I'm worried about dieying*
 -I am worried about my grades.
– *The thing i'm worried about is my family get covid-19.*
– *Something i'm worried about is my family, 3 family members from mexico died in the past week.*
– *There's nothing i'm worried about.*

MY INSIGHTS
Many students are very worried and I am so glad that they felt comfortable enough to share some of them with me. I know some students are very worried, but are still not willing to share. Since they are listening to the discussion, it will help them tremendously anyway.

When I read, "I'm worried about dieying," I knew it was a red flag so I put everyone in a breakout room and had a discussion with this child. She is not afraid of getting sick and she does NOT want to hurt herself. She said that she is worried about dying because she will not see her mom anymore, that it will be dark, and that scares her. She was so open, honest, and willing to share because she needed someone to hear her and she has been dealing with this for a long time.

I sent an email to the principal to see if she can get counseling. In the meantime, I gave her a few suggestions, in an email (so she would not forget our discussion).

My email to her:
"If you do these things, I think it will REALLY help.
1. Breathe into the area of your brain that feels uncomfortable. Deeply and slowly.
2. When you are trying to fall asleep, breathe deeply and let it out slowly at least 20 times or until you fall asleep. Breathing deeply slows down all of that talking in your brain.
3. Catch it! Every time you feel uncomfortable, catch it and breathe.
4. When you notice the discomfort in your brain, pretend to sit in the middle of the icky feeling.
5. Don't fight with your emotions. Just notice them. Don't try to change them."

Student's email: *"ok and It's a blessing to have you come in my life to try and help me and I just wanted to say thank you for the help bc in don't really like to share my emotions with people because some do care but some people ignore me when I tell then these things."*

My email to her: "You are so sweet, kind, and special. I hope you can dissolve this quickly!!!! It may take some time, but it will dissolve. I will keep emailing you to see how you are.

Sometimes people seem to ignore you when you share these things and it's usually because they don't know what to say and it's easier for

them to just ignore. I know it doesn't feel good but some people just don't understand and they are doing the best they can. "
    Meditation: Serene Mind

QUESTION
What can you do if you get worried?
Actual student responses (without any corrections)
- *I can go to fall asleep and forget everything.*
- *I can think of the positive things instead.*
- *what I do is take a walk or use my bike to get fresh air.*
- *When I am stressed I can play with my pets*
- *talk to my family and try to prevent the worry from coming back*
- *Take deep breaths.*
- *just try to forget about it*
- *I can try to take a deep breath and try to foucuse on what is going on now and not the future*
- *I clam my self down or i take a nap to forget every thing*
- *Play video games*
- *When I am worried I paint of watch movies.*
- *I like to paint and draw.*
- *Try not to think about it as much.*
- *Sometimes what I do when i'm worried is play video games to get that out of my mind*
- *I try to think about the positive sides.*
- *When I am worried I light a lavender candle that I have in my room and I do something calming like playing the piano or knitting.*
- *I watch funny videos or watch something that will make me forget about it for a while*

MY INSIGHTS
    I assumed that students knew what to do when the stressful feeling of worry came up, and I was wrong again. I am so glad that I continue to connect by asking questions and that they are so willing to share. I honestly

thought that the students would say, "catch it, breathe, and it dissolves" since I have said it so often. I was shocked to read that they would paint, draw, ride a bike, think of the positive, watch movies, just try to forget it, or go to sleep. Not surprisingly, as avoiding discomfort is what most adults do. This is just a habit we have all fallen into because it feels "normal." This is NOT a judgement of anyone; merely an observation. Until I had this knowledge, it was normal for me to avoid any discomfort by grabbing a pizza and watching lots and lots of TV. It is a habit that I learned to break and the first step was to be aware of how I was feeling.

I also shared that avoiding the icky feeling is easier than feeling it, BUT the problem is that it will go away only temporarily. The feeling will come back, and it will come back stronger. So, when the feeling comes up, if we don't want it to come back stronger, we need to become aware in the moment. No one wants fear, doubt, or frustration to come back stronger.

Again, in order to be free of worry (or any stressful feeling), first be aware of it when it is happening, breathe, and it will dissolve in time. If there is time, we can also meditate. Please know that there are other "techniques" for adults who are struggling to dissolve their stressful state. The focus of this book is for children and young adults who are, for the most part, dealing with less stress than most adults. However, this is a perfect place for everyone to start.

Meditation: One minute breathing with eyes open

January 27, 2021 (Week 21 of School – Distance Learning)

QUESTION
How are you feeling right now?
Actual student responses (without any corrections)

– *calm*
– *nervous*
– *annoyed*
– *confused*

– uneasy
– happy
– happy
– happy
– confident
– I feel scared

MY INSIGHTS

I have not asked this question in a while and I just wanted to check in with them. I was pleasantly surprised to see how many said that they were happy. I am also impressed that their vocabulary is expanding when they are sharing their discomfort. I really liked the word, "uneasy," because it is how I feel from time to time and I did not have a good word to describe it.

QUESTION

How can you get rid of your stressful feelings?

Actual student responses (without any corrections)

– catch it
– Mediate
– Take deep breaths
– I'm just going to focus more on what I need to focused.
– I can fix it by taking deep breaths.
– You can fix it by catching it.
– I could take deep breaths
– I will catch it.

MY INSIGHTS

I asked this question because yesterday we talked a LOT about not avoiding what we are feeling and I wanted to see how much the students retained. I am pleasantly surprised that they now know to catch it, breathe, and meditate. We will be reviewing this at least once a week.

Meditation: One minute breathing with eyes open

January 28, 2021 (Week 21 of School – Distance Learning)

QUESTION

Do you think that if you worry about something it will change
the outcome?

Actual student responses (without any corrections)

– *No*

– *Yes.*

– *yes*

– *No*

– *yes*

– *no*

– *yes*

- *Yes*

– *No*

– *yes*

– *Yes*

– *yes*

– *yes*

– *no*

– *yes it will*

– *Yes?*

MY INSIGHTS

Not what I expected. So many students thought that if they worry about something, it will change the outcome. This led into a great and deep discussion.

QUESTION

Please explain how worrying will change the outcome.

Actual student responses (without any corrections)

– *Nothing will change because if you get worried that's not going to fix the problem*

– *I will change because the person would feel under pressure and would not know what to do.*

– *Worrying will change the outcome because you will not help because your busy worrying*

– *If I worry it'll change the outcome because I start getting very worried and get distracted*

– *It will make it worse because then you will be stressed.*

– *It wont change it because people can't change outcomes it just happens.*

– *I won't change the situation for them but it might make it worse for you because being stressed isn't healthy.*

– *It will not change it because your just worrying about it and you have to take action if not your gonna be very stressed.*

– *It will not change anything because if you keep worry and don't do anything about it you will just make you feel worse and worry even more and it will affect you more than any other person or thing you are worrying about.*

– *the situation won't change it because it is not under my control and it can make it worse for me as i may not be able to function because of all of this extra stress and anxiety.*

MY INSIGHTS

After reading their statements, I realized that they many did not understand what "outcome" meant. Their focus was on how worrying would affect their own self, which is actually incredibly important. Most already knew that stress is not healthy.

I told them that if they do or do not worry, it will not change the outcome of a situation. They have to calm themselves down, get into a beautiful, peaceful state, and then solutions will come to them. If they are stressed and worried, there is not space for solutions to "jump" into their brain. Once they are calm, it is amazing what ideas come to them. They did not fully understand what I was trying to teach them, so I shared a real life example that happened to me.

I brought the discussion up about worrying because of something that happened to me yesterday. I was worried that the students were not practicing enough math problems and I caught it and sat in the worry (while the students were in breakout rooms). I got myself calm and a solution came to me. I had a HUGE smile on my face because it was something that I could do that I had not thought of yet. The students are in groups of three to four already. They will go to breakout rooms to do a math problem and come back to the main room when they all agree. They will have to work together which means they will learn more. I loved that I was able to catch that I was worried, that I calmed myself down, and an amazing solution came. I shared this with the students, and now they believe that it works, because it does.

Meditation: Serene Mind

QUESTION
What did you get from this conversation about being worried?
Actual student responses (without any corrections)
– *That worrying about a person won't change anything.*
– *Being worried is not going to help you.*
– *I know that if you are worried you get stressed.*
– *I learned that worrying is not going to help me.*
– *That whether you worry or not, you simply cannot help the problem and it won't change the outcome*
– *That even when your worried it won't change the outcome*
– *Worrying will not affect the ending.*
– *Worrying won't change anything unless you take action.*

– I learned that worrying won't help at all it will just make it worse for myself.

MY INSIGHTS

I love that they were starting to realize that worrying does not help the outcome and that a solution will come to them when they are calm.
Meditation: Serene Mind

February 1, 2021 (Week 22 of School – Distance Learning)

QUESTION

Tell me two things that you are willing to do this week to help you learn better.
Actual student responses (without any corrections)
– Try to do my homework earlier and pay more attention in class.
– I can focus more and not get distracted by other things.
– I can't think of anything I'm willing to do
– I am willing to avoid any type of distractions and focus more.
– I am willing to pay attention in class and do my work.
– Two things that I am willing to do this week to help me learn better are listen/pay attention to class and only worry about what we are doing at that moment.
– I am willing to put more attention and effort to my school work
– Really anything I don't mind doing anything as long as it helps me learn.

MY INSIGHTS

I wanted the students to write down some ideas to help them learn this week. I read many of the shares aloud so that the students, who are not doing well, could see that they were not alone. If they see that others are struggling too, in my experience it helps them to not give up. This question was another example of students connecting with other students. I've also noticed that not only are the students able to share their emotions with me, their overall writing is getting much better.

QUESTION

What do you think the difference is between learning and grades?

Actual student responses (without any corrections)

– *Learning is fun grades are stressful.*

– *learning is getting educated and grades are the rewards you get*

– *People can learn but have no intentions in doing any work.*

– *Learning is absorbing information into your brain and grades are the result of that*

– *Grades dont really help sometimes they stress you out/ With learning actually helps you with math, reading, and all of that.*

– *Learning is when I learn and grades are just how well or bad I did but it's also like a reflection on what I need to work on.*

– *For me grades are important but not really because what's important are the things I learn and not how what score I get.*

– *The difference between learning and grades is that learning is nice I like it but on the other hand grades are exhausting and it's hard working.*

MY INSIGHTS

I LOVED this discussion. Many students understood the definition of learning and grades but did not really "get it." Sometimes a grade does not reflect what a student really knows. A student can be failing math because they have not done the homework or classwork, but has learned a lot nonetheless. Sometimes a student can have an A in math but has learned very little because they have cheated their way to an A. Because of distance learning, I know (and have caught) several students cheating.

So, I said to them, YEAH, you have an A in middle school math. . . . So? Did you learn it? I don't have any control over your cheating because that is your decision. Again, you got an A in middle school math. Did you learn the prerequisites needed to pass high school algebra? Wait, but you got an A in middle school math. When you apply for college, do they care that you got an A in middle school math or do they care that you learned the information? I kept saying in a "joking way", "Yes! You got an A in middle school math but did you learn it?" to help them see the importance of learning and trying.

I keep telling the students that the most important thing about learning is to make mistakes and learn from them. If today, you get twelve out of twenty-five correct, then tomorrow you get thirteen out of twenty-five, you are learning. After this discussion, I have noticed that they are turning in many more assignments.

QUESTION
How does cheating affect your life?
Actual student responses (without any corrections)

– *Cheating now will affect you later.*
– *If we cheat we are gonna mess up high school*
– *Don't cheat unless you don't want to learn.*
– *You need to learn and not cheat.*
– *That its better to do the work than not doing it or cheating. Its better to try and learn it than to not learn it and to then cheat.*
– *people are doing the work but not learning and that will hurt every part of future*
– *To not cheat because if you do then you will end up cheating forever since you won't know what to do.*
– *Even if you get an A but you cheat your grade doesn't matter. If you cheat now it would be be hard for the rest of our lives.*

MY INSIGHTS
I wanted to see how much they really took away from the conversation. Many of my students are the first generation to go to college. I want them to start thinking about the decisions they are making now so that they are prepared for higher education. Every decision they make affects their future.

FINAL THOUGHTS

It has been about a year since we have been in the pandemic and doing distance learning and I am noticing that teaching is becoming MUCH easier. I KNOW the students are learning and it is ALL because of the emotional connection we have cultivated in the last twenty-two weeks. It is NOT easy but, with this strong bond, teaching and learning has been doable. Of course, being in the building is so much easier.

Today in class, I sat back and watched the students answer math questions and share emotions in the chat. I had tears in my eyes. We have connected at a deep level, and I believe that the majority of the students will come out of the pandemic confident, calm, and with a strong grasp of math. I am so proud of them.

I also realized that I do not HAVE to ask them so many questions to get them to open up since the connection is there. Many students have been emailing me after class to share things like this: their brother was having a hard time breathing and had to go to the hospital, their dog had puppies, their grandfather is sick, etc.. I will continue to ask questions and share ways to help them through their stressful emotions.

In order to help more students, I HAVE to share this information with as many teachers as possible. Today, I had a discussion with some teachers who did not understand why their students were not talking in the breakout rooms. They sounded frustrated and I knew that feeling very well because I went through it eighteen weeks ago.

I gave some suggestions that worked beautifully for my students. In a nutshell, they will need to: go slowly, ask students often how they are feeling, give them questions to talk about not related to school, let them choose the people in their group, and share in the chat often. The students are not comfortable or connected to other students in the same grade, so they are scared to share and be vulnerable.

In the next meeting, I will share with the teachers that if students (and teachers) can become aware of their feelings, and breathe, the "icky" emotions will not be so strong and they will be more comfortable to share. It also makes teaching much easier and fun. It has worked for me. If the teachers can see the success of my students, they may be more willing to try it.

TEACHING TOOLS

CONNECTION TECHNIQUES
Do's and Don'ts for Teachers

"We have not paid attention to our inner state. We never thought it was important to live in a beautiful state. This has not been a part of our formal education, but it needs to be."

– Krishnaji, Co-founder of O & O Academy

- Be aware of the need for connection

- Use your intuition when asking questions. You may be prompted to ask a question you didn't know you would ask. The students will be aware of scripted questions and will not reply as naturally.

- Listen and let the students know you are listening by your honest feedback

- Be easy on yourself in this process

- Go slow but be very consistent with the questions and meditations-it's a journey

- Introduce meditation -- very short ones at the beginning

- Have them share their meditation experience each time they do it

- Be in the moment and show students how to do the same and repeat often

- Discuss feeling and be aware of them throughout the day

- Include homework at times about catching emotions

- Notice how the students are more engaged in class

- Be ready for your assumptions to be wrong about how students feel

- Be ready for their shares to break your heart and make you cry

- Be ready to flow from question to question with very little teaching for that day

- Go easy on yourself. If you start with connecting, the year of teaching becomes much easier for all involved.

- Don't judge their answers because they are sharing what they actually feel

- Include words of encouragement to help young people through a difficult situation when needed

- Praise often and genuinely

- When a child is obviously mad or frustrated, don't ask them what's wrong but ask them if they caught the emotion. Focus on the feeling, not the why.

- DO NOT TRY TO FIX ALL OF THEIR "PROBLEMS" – just listen

- If the questions don't flow easily, you may need come back to them later. Don't force it.

- Teach them NOT TO AVOID or TO JUDGE an emotion but to notice it, catch it, breathe and then it starts to dissolve.

- This is NOT positive thinking.

- Ask how they are feeling often so that it can become second nature.

- Share similar comments without their names so that the group knows that they are not alone in what they are feeling.

- Share pertinent things from your life to help connect even further.

- When you think you have connected enough and want to stop, don't. This continues throughout the year.

- Acknowledge the students growth with being able to verbalize their feelings.

- Encourage the students to teach their parents about what they are learning about their feelings.

- Notice how each class starts to be more connected as they often share the same feelings.

- It's ok to ask different questions to each class as long as they flow

- If you as the adult are feeling tired, frustrated of uneasy, use that to see if the children are feeling the same way or have felt that way before.

- If you get stuck and can't think of a question, ask the students for some examples.

- You can ask about a specific emotion and see what their thoughts are

- Know that the time spent talking is NOT a waste of time. Students are hurting and you may be the only person that has asked them how they are feeling. It's important.

- Help them break the fear of failing

- Ask the question that comes to your mind

- Talk about stress, anger, fear of abandonment, pressure so it's not taboo for the student

- Have one on one conversations when needed

- Teach (stressful emotions) icky feeling and (calm) beautiful feelings

"All humanity lives in only 2 states of being . . .
A SUFFERING STATE OR A BEAUTIFUL STATE.
There is no 3rd state."
– Krishnaji, Co-founder of O & O Academy

- Teach them how to breath-in and out their nose-breathe in deeply and let it out slowly.

- Focus on things not related to school also

- Recognize YOUR own feelings

- Have students catch "icky" feeling and beautiful feelings for homework for more practice

It has been my honor to write this book and to be able to share it with you. Please remember that connecting with children is an ALL year long process, whether the students are in distance learning on Zoom or in a classroom setting. Connecting with my students has been the most important thing that I did with them because it made them felt safe enough to learn. Teaching the core curriculum came second (with an unexpected outcome of tremendous learning). I wish you all the best in your journey of connection, and in your joy of teaching.

*Reader of this book: I encourage you to notice your own emotions and not run from them. The more that you can grow in catching your feelings and dissolve them, the easier it will be to teach your students.

If you want any additional information on meditations, joining meditations (so you can become an expert at Serene Mind), O & O Academy, or if you have any other questions, please contact me at hearusnow2020@gmail.com or go to O&O Academy's web site: ekam.org

APPENDIX A

MEDITATIONS

One minute listening: The students close their eyes, stay as still as they can, and just listen. They breathe in deeply and let it out slowly. Start with one minute. After a few weeks, increase it to two minutes, then to three minutes.

Breathe deeply with open eyes: The students breathe in deeply and let it out slowly five times. This can be done before a test or when something bothers them and they cannot stop and close their eyes.

Breathe deeply with closed eyes: The students breathe in deeply and let it out slowly five times. This can be done before a test or when they feel an "icky" state and if they are able to close their eyes.

Serene Mind Meditation

I have done this meditation many times for myself and became an expert before I did it with students. I lead it myself with kid-friendly language instead of having them listen to it.

Preethaji (2018). Serene Mind. Retrieved from https://www.youtube.com/watch?v=OXg8xcWBMuo.

This is how I lead it:

Breathe in deeply and let it out slowly. [I say this three to five times.] Notice how you feel in this exact moment. Do you feel annoyed, frustrated, angry, or do you feel calm and happy? Just notice it, don't judge it or try to change it.

Now, let your thoughts wander. They may take you to the past or to the future. Just see where your mind takes you. [One minute]

Now, visualize a tiny candle flame between your eyebrows. See that tiny flame slide into the center of your brain and focus on that flame for a few moments. [Twenty seconds]

Take a deep breath in, slowly let it out, and put a gentle smile on your face.

Take another deep breath in, slowly let it out, and gently open your eyes.

[Total time: three to four minutes]

Gratitude Meditation: https://www.breathingroom.com/videos/feel gratitude [I modify it for children and I guide it.]

Gratitude Meditation

From O & O Academy, modified for students.

Close your eyes, please. Breathe in deeply and exhale slowly. Stay as still as you can. Focus fully on your breath.

Today we will do a gratitude meditation. There have been so many people in the world who have helped us. Some we know, and some we don't. Let's begin.

Hold in your thoughts one person who has nurtured you in your childhood. It could be a parent, family member, neighbor, or even a pet. [Pause for about 30 seconds.]

Thank that person for being a part of your life.
Wish for their wellbeing.

Think of one person who has inspired you to be a better human being.
Thank that person for being a part of your life. [Pause.]

Wish for their wellbeing.

Think of one person who has made you feel wanted and loved.

Thank that person for being a part of your life. [Pause.]
Wish for their wellbeing.

Think of one person who is helping you or encouraging you with school. Thank that person for being a part of your life. [Pause.]
Wish for their wellbeing.

Think of Mother Earth; feel her in your heart. Think of what she has done for you. For example: air to breathe, plants for oxygen, water for drinking.

Thank her for sustaining and upholding your existence. Thank her for everything she has done for you even though you have never noticed it before.
Wish for her wellbeing.

Take a deep breath in, and slowly let it out, and put a gentle smile on your face. Take another deep breath in, and gently open your eyes.

APPENDIX B

DEFINITIONS OF STRESSFUL AND BEAUTIFUL STATES ACCORDING TO TWELVE-YEAR-OLDS

STRESSFUL STATES (FEELINGS AND EMOTIONS)

QUESTION

List the stressful emotions that you have felt. List when you have felt icky, stressed or yuck.

Actual student responses (without some spelling corrections) *a bad human being, a burden, a menace, afraid, alone, anger, angry, annoyed, anxiety, anxious, ashamed, bashful, blue, bossed around, breakdown, breaking down, broken, Broken down, challenged, cold, confused, denial, depression, depressed, disappointed, discouraged, disgust, disgusted, distress, distress, down, drained, dumb, embarrassed, emotionless, emotional, empty, enclosed, enraged, failed, failure, falling apart, fearful, feel like a loser, feel without a heart, feeling down, feeling like trash, frightened, frustrated, frustration, furious, garbage, giving up, gloomy, grief, grumpiness, guilt, guilty, gullible, hangry, hated, hateful, helpless, hopeless, hurt, icky, idiot, ignored, immature, in the way of everyone, Insecure, irresponsible, irritability, irritated, like I need to protect myself from everyone, livid, lonely, lost, lost in my own mind, mad, menace, miserable, misunderstood, nervous, not confident, not confident in myself, not good enough, not worth it, numb, outcaste, overthinking, overwhelmed, pain, pointless, pointless is like you aren't important, procrastinating, punching bag, rejected, restlessness, rushed, sad, sadness, scared, self-conscious, shattered, shy, sick, smad, sorrow, stressed, stupid, tired, traumatized, troublemaker, troubled, turned down, uncomfortable, unfocused, ungrateful, unhappy, unneeded, unsecured, untrusted, unuseful, unwanted, upset, useless, weak, without purpose, worthless, your fault*

BEAUTIFUL STATES (FEELINGS, EMOTIONS)

QUESTION
List some beautiful feeling that you have experienced.

Actual student responses (without some spelling corrections) *adventurous, amazed, angel, awesome, beautiful, blessed, brave, brave, bubbly, calm, caring, cheerful, chill, comfortable, confidence, confident, content and cheerful, cool, ecstatic, empathy, encouraged, energetic, energized, enthusiastic, excited, exuberant, fabulous, faithful, fearless, feel like I can do anything, fortunate, friendship, full of life, funny, generous, genius, gleeful, good, grateful, gratitude, happiness, happy, heavenly, helpful, hope, hopeful, in peace, independent, invincible, jolly, joy, joyful, kind, kindness, knowing, knowledgeable, laughter, like earning money for the first time by working, lovable, love, loved, lucky, merry, motivated, needed, non-stressed, not alone, not embarrassed, not lonely, noticed, over joyed, owning a house, peaceful, positive, powerful, pride, proud, recognized, relaxed, relieved, respected, respectful, rested, safe, satisfied, self-acceptance, selfless, showing pleasure, smart, strong, sweet, talented, the feeling that you did something right and that you are happy, thoughtful, thrilled, trust, trusted, unstoppable, useful, wanted, warm, welcomed, wonderful, you just did something new, your having fun I done know what it's called*

If you want any additional information on meditations, joining meditations (so you can become an expert at Serene Mind), O & O Academy, or if you have any other questions, please contact me at hearusnow2020@gmail.com

www.ingramcontent.com/pod-product-compliance
Lightning Source LLC
Chambersburg PA
CBHW061950070426
42450CB00007BA/1112

9 781736 991602